A Wee Dram

Also by David Daiches

Scotch Whisky: its Past and Present
Glasgow
A Study of Literature
God and the Poets
The Idea of a New University
Robert Burns
Some Late Victorian Attitudes
Robert Fergusson
Two Worlds: An Edinburgh Jewish Childhood
Edinburgh: A Traveller's Companion
Edinburgh
Scotland and the Union
Bonnie Prince Charlie

A Wee Dram

DRINKING SCENES FROM
SCOTTISH LITERATURE

David Daiches

ANDRE DEUTSCH

First published in Great Britain 1990
by André Deutsch Limited
105−106 Great Russell Street, London WC1

British Library Cataloguing in Publication Data
A Wee Dram.
  1. English literature. Scottish writers. Special subjects.
  Whiskies, Scotch consumption anthologies
  I. Daiches, David, *1912−*
  820.80355

ISBN 0 233 98602 2

Printed and bound in Great Britain by
Butler & Tanner Ltd Frome Somerset

Contents

5

Introduction

A dram is originally a measure of weight for liquids (a quarter of a fluid ounce): the word is first found as meaning a small drink of spirits at the end of the fifteenth century and since then it has become universally associated with the Scot and his whisky. Scotland and whisky, like freedom and whisky in Burns's famous phrase, 'gang thegither'. Ever since the great Scotch whisky entrepreneurs of the late nineteenth century – Haig, Dewar, Walker, Buchanan and Mackie – promoted Scotch whisky as a world drink, it has, paradoxically, been universally associated with Scotsmen. Scotsmen, not Scotswomen. Whisky has traditionally been a male drink in Scotland. In the years just after the last war when my wife and I spent our summers among her farming relatives in north-east Scotland, I was always offered a dram when I arrived at the farmhouse (whatever the time of day) but my wife was given sherry. The late Sir Herbert Grierson, who was my professor at the University of Edinburgh, once told me of an incident when he was a newly married man recently appointed to the Chair of English at Aberdeen. His wife was giving her first dinner party to honour the great Professor George Saintsbury, visiting from Edinburgh. As the maid was serving pre-prandial drinks, Professor Saintsbury, that notable connoisseur of wines and spirits as well as of English and French literature, rose from his chair and came across the room to where Grierson was sitting. 'I think you ought to know,' he said, 'that your maid is serving whisky under the impression that it is sherry. It doesn't bother me, but it may trouble the ladies.'

The popular association of whisky with Scotland is in a sense misleading. The traditional drink of Lowland Scots for centuries was ale or beer, and beer is still the main drink in a Scottish pub, sometimes preceded by a dram of whisky, though the consumption of what in Edinburgh used to be called 'a nip and a pint' is now fairly rare. Whisky was, however, the traditional Highland drink, as the Gaelic origin of the word – *uisge beatha*, or water of life – makes clear. Whisky of a kind was distilled in the Lowlands as early as the seventeenth century and in a few individual cases earlier, but it was in the Highlands that the great tradition of pot-still malt whisky (made from malted barley dried in the smoke of a peat fire) had flourished from very early times, eventually to reach out to the Lowlands in the eighteenth and nineteenth centuries.

In the eighteenth century claret, imported directly from Bordeaux to Leith, was the great drink among gentlemen, and there are innumerable stories of the claret-drinking prowess of the legal luminaries of that century, of 'four-bottle men' who would consume four bottles at a sitting, of judges sipping claret on the bench or appearing in court in the morning after a night spent in the continuous consumption of claret miraculously in full possession of their faculties. If eighteenth-century Scottish gentlemen wanted spirits, it would more likely be brandy than whisky that they took. The smuggling of brandy from France to Scotland was as much of a worry to the Government as the illicit distilling of whisky in the Highlands.

Ordinary folk, however, did not drink claret: they drank the product not of the grape but of barley. Both ale and whisky were (and are) made from barley, and in his poem 'Scotch Drink' Burns praises both the products of that cereal:

> Let other poets raise a fracas
> 'Bout vines and wines an' drucken Bacchus,
> An' crabbed names and stories wrack us,
>   An' grate our lug.
> I sing the juice Scotch bear can mak us
>   In glass or jug.

> O thou, my Muse! guid auld SCOTCH DRINK!
> Whether thro' wimplin worms thou jink
> Or, richly brown, ream owre the brink,
>   In glorious faem,
> Inspire me till I lisp and wink
>   To sing thy name.

'Bear' is barley. Burns is hailing the juice of the barley of both kinds – ale or beer, which froths richly brown in glorious foam, and whisky, which passes through 'wimplin worms' (twisting pipes) in the process of distillation. It is beer that Tam o' Shanter drinks, 'reaming swats' (foaming beer) that drank divinely. He was 'bousing at the nappy' (ale). Burns's Jolly Beggars, who met in Poosie Nansie's inn, drank whisky, but it was the inferior Lowland Kilbagie, not the real Highland malt whisky, which Burns relished when he could get it.

When Lowlanders drank whisky in the eighteenth century they usually made it into toddy (whisky, hot water and sugar) or punch (whisky, hot water, sugar and lemon). In Glasgow, where the eighteenth-century

10

'Tobacco Lords' made fortunes from importing tobacco from Virginia, and rum from the West Indies was a staple import, their standard drink was rum or rum punch.

Drinking in Scotland, whether of beer, whisky, rum or claret, is generally associated with scenes of conviviality. It took place in taverns, pubs, private houses and in the open air. It accompanied funerals as well as weddings. It was associated with a great variety of social rituals, of consolation as well as celebration, of companionship as well as parting. After the Distillery Act of 1825, aimed at eliminating illicit distilling and in the process reducing the excise tax on whisky, legal whisky became relatively cheap and as the century progressed it became increasingly the solace of those victims of the industrial revolution who struggled on low wages in an atmosphere of urban squalor. It provided a short cut if not to happiness at least to oblivion. The association of whisky drinking with squalid living and ruined families was the theme of many a 'total abstinence' propagandist in Victorian Glasgow and many an earnest churchman and political reformer fought against the evils of drink throughout the nineteenth century. But during and immediately after the First World War the duty on whisky was steadily increased and the poor man's road to temporary oblivion was cut off. The music-hall song 'Twelve and a tanner a bottle' was a response to the increase in the price of a bottle of whisky from four shillings at the beginning of the First World War to twelve shillings and sixpence immediately afterwards. 'How can a fellow be happy, if happiness costs such a lot?' the song ended, a sad commentary on the misuse of a great spirit.

The increasingly discriminating drinking of single malt whiskies (rather than blends) has been a feature of the last decade, and the abuse of liquor is now more commonly associated with the ingestion of large quantities of lager (a relatively new drink to Scotland) by young males. The availability of lager in cans, easily transported to any public or private place, has exacerbated this problem. But this takes us far from traditional kinds of drinking in Scotland. As presented to us in literature, the wee dram as well as the foaming mug of ale or beer or the bottle of claret is the accompaniment of some of the most significant aspects of social life, both happy and unhappy, and as such it tells an eloquent story.

Finally, a word about drink and weather. The Scottish poets were the first to tell the truth about the weather in the British Isles. Where mediaeval English poets were celebrating beautiful May mornings (and Chaucer's pilgrims didn't get wet even in an English April), the Scots were describing rough scenes of winter weather in town and country. The two great 'makars' of the fifteenth century, Robert Henryson and William Dunbar, as well as the fifteenth-to-sixteenth century Gavin Douglas, have some splendid descriptions of Scottish winters. It is Henryson who makes the connection between cold weather and drinking. As the wind howls outside he makes up the fire and pours himself a drink:

> I mend the fyre, and beikit me about,
> Than tuik ane drink my spreitis to comfort.

The drink he took to comfort his spirits is not identified, but it is interesting that about the time that Henryson was composing this poem, *The Testament of Cresseid*, we find the first recorded allusion in the Scottish Exchequer Rolls to malt supplied for the making of *aquavitae*, water of life, i.e., *uisge beatha* or whisky. I think we may assume that this was the comforting liquor taken by Henryson, and that his poetry gives us the first recorded wee dram in Scottish literature.

Neil M. Gunn

The First Dram

Neil Gunn (1891–1973), the distinguished Scottish novelist, was an excise officer from 1911 to 1937 and spent much of his time in distilleries. His book *Whisky and Scotland*, first published in 1935, is largely a lively and witty argument in favour of single malt whiskies and against blends: it is a pioneer work and a classic in the literature of whisky. The book opens with this wholly imaginary account of the accidental discovery of whisky.

Whisky comes from the Gaelic *uisge-beatha* meaning 'water of life.' In the curious mind this will at once rouse wonder, perhaps even a contemplative effort to surprise the ancestral thought in its creative moment. For clearly there is nothing haphazard or transitory about the designation. It was not coined for the slang or commerce of any age. Rather is it akin to one of the ultimate elements into which ancient philosophers resolved the universe. It is not a description so much as a simple statement of truth and of mystery.

Is it now possible to conceive by what process some long-dead mouth and tongue were led to breathe out the magic syllables upon the liquor's aftermath?

Down round the southern corner of the *dun* there was a field of barley all ripened by the sun. In a small wind it echoed faintly the sound of the ocean; at night it sighed and rustled as the earth mother thought over things, not without a little anxiety. It was cut and harvested and a sheaf offered in thanksgiving; flailed and winnowed; until the ears of grain remained in a heap of pale gold: the bread of life.

In simple ways the grain was prepared and ground and set to ferment; the fermented liquor was then boiled, and as the steam came off it was by happy chance condensed against some cold surface.

And lo! this condensation of the steam from the greenish-yellow fermented gruel is clear as crystal. It is purer than any water from any well. When cold, it is colder to the fingers than ice.

A marvellous transformation. A perfect water. But in the mouth – what is this? The gums tingle, the throat burns, down into the belly fire passes, and thence outward to the finger-tips, to the feet, and finally to the head.

13

The man was a bit tired, exasperated a little, for things had been going wrong (how often they must have gone wrong with the primitive experimenter!), and, for the rest – or he wouldn't have been at the job – not a little weary with the dulness of social life, including the looks of women and the ambitions of fools.

And then – and then – the head goes up. The film dissolves from the eyes; they glisten. He abruptly laughs and jumps to his feet; as abruptly pauses to look over himself with a marvelling scrutiny. He tries the muscles of his arms. They are full of such energy that one fist shoots out; then the other. A right and left. His legs have the same energy. He begins to dance with what is called primitive abandon. Clearly it was not water he had drunk: *it was life*.

I know this is rather a poetic reconstruction, to be regarded with proper amusement, yet it is difficult to understand any history without some exercise of the imagination. What meaning can a human fact have until it is comprehended in thought and feeling? Let us pursue the method a little further.

Aware that he had achieved an 'epoch-making discovery,' his first impulse would be to communicate it to his friends. Again the cynical interpreter of history may doubt this; but here even recorded fact is with us overwhelmingly. For illicit distillation today, not only in the remote wastes of our mountains and glens but in our cities, could be carried on to a very great extent without much fear of direct discovery by revenue officials, were it not that in one form or another 'information is received'. Sometimes this information is deliberately conveyed, more often it is overheard. And even when deliberately conveyed, the motive is rarely or never one of pecuniary gain, but nearly always the satisfaction of some passion, thwarted or jealous or righteous. This might be illustrated with a recent instance which has come to my knowledge. Three men are standing at the public bar of an inn in one of the wildest and remotest places of Britain. They are drinking whisky, and having paid good money for it they are disposed to be critical. For it would appear they know better stuff than this. This stuff is watered to nothing and pretty rotten at that! They smile to each other knowingly. They wink. They ask the barman if this is the best he can do for them. Does he call this the real Mackay? They are a society getting fun out of their secret knowledge and urged to gloat over it by subtle innuendo. They give nothing directly away, of course. Indeed they would suffer any penalty rather than do that. But one traveller who is there, quietly having a drink by himself, overhears and wonders. He passes on the story and a few months later an illicit still is captured.

The first impulse, then, in the original discoverer would be to communicate with his friends. It is not impossible, however, that before actually setting off he tried his life-water again, just to make sure that he had not been a victim of some unusual form of witchery. It is even possible that as a scientist he considered it his duty to use his own body for further experimental purposes. While the poet would have arisen and gone singing through the forest at once, the scientist nobly prepares to sacrifice himself in the interests of knowledge.

Studying his reactions to a second draught, he would find that he had not been mistaken. Moreover, to the early ecstatic feelings there now supervened a state of consciousness marked by extreme mental clarity. Problems that had worried him for a long time, touching affairs of the family and the tribe, were seen in their true light, proportionately, and for what they were worth. And problems touching in particular the validity of certain religious aspects of totemic belief were seen to contain elements that were – peculiar. Decidedly peculiar. He smiled – to the liquor, which was of the ineffable transparency of truth. Another little test wouldn't do him any harm. . . . In this way, and as one of the first martyrs to science, he slowly 'passed out'.

But, like similar martyrs of a succeeding age, he would recover by-and-by, when, more than ever, he would desire to communicate with his friends, for what had been lost in initial eagerness would now be replaced with wisdom and a certain penetential awe.

His friends, his bosom cronies, would be more than taken in a little by this profound, even sad sense of experience, with its air of earnest secrecy. They had always said that one day he would go a bit too far; that some demon would possess him whom no druid could expel. Yet they liked him and so went privily with him through the woods to the small hill stream, taking care that neither Druid nor Chief saw them, and, in particular, that no scent of their intention crossed the nostrils of the Elders.

Yes, he admitted, that was the stuff, and he began to tell them how he had made it.

They scoffed. What, that well water! They drank.

Two of them revealed a rivalry which had hardly been suspected before, even by themselves. They fought. A man with a grey beard regarded a far horizon with eyes in which the light of an infinite under-standing and kindliness shone. 'Stop them fighting,' he said, 'I want to talk.' But there was a man there who, though a bard, happened also to be trustworthy, and he started singing.

Meantime the Discoverer had at last helped himself, and presently the dull ache in his head was dispelled and a prompting to dance was balanced by a divine quiescence. Carefully he carried what was left of the liquor over beside the old man. 'Would you like another little drop?' he asked. 'Well, if you make it a small one,' replied the old man, who nevertheless was so taken with this magic drink that he helped himself to a stout measure. 'Canny!' shouted the Bard at him, interrupting his song to do so. And the fighters, catching the anxiety in the Bard's voice, called each other fools in strong language and joined the Bard.

As the sun went down they swore an immortal fellowship. The two fighters pricked their little fingers and ritually sealed a blood-brother-hood. But as for the rest of the world, not a word! Hush!

The atmosphere they carried about with them, however, was thick enough to stop a poisoned arrow. And at the very next distilling, the Elders surprised them.

So this was what all the mysterious silences and looks and enigmatic boastings – and smell – had been about! This was the unholy brew!

And just here – for all this may not be entirely irrelevant – it should be made clear that this folk were founded on what they called the democratic principle; that is to say, they believed that power ultimately resided in themselves, but for the smooth working of their community in peace and war, they found it convenient to elect Elders, a religious teacher or Druid, and a leader or Chief. It will thus be seen that they were a very primitive people; indeed so primitive that they were even prepared to fight for this democratic principle of theirs. And if that may seem obscure to many good Europeans now, still an effort should be made to understand it, were it only for this odd reason, namely, that it has persisted with an astonishing force among the elements of that folk to this day. In seeking the reason for so strange a survival, even we may find ourselves compelled to dip into the well of the water of life.

During which time the Elders had drunk.

The others, including the Discoverer, watched and waited. No one had ever seen an Elder dance. Their eyes glistened unholily.

But the eyes of the Elders batted no eyelid. True, as the life-water had gone round, each had emitted a curious lengthy sound like a half-strangled cough. In after times this sound became well known, but then it was still young and charged with humorous surprise. To offset this expression, however, the Elders' faces immediately became unusually grave. Slowly each drew his hand down his beard, while his brows ridged in thought. They sat in a sun circle, which has neither prece-dence nor disruption, beginning nor end. As the life-water was making its third circuit, the Bard, who was prone to impatience, asked them for their finding.

They meditated in silence yet awhile, then the oldest Elder (they had the unbiological custom of respecting age) declared they had decided to take the matter to avizandum.

'What matter?' demanded the Bard.

'This matter,' responded the Elder, pointing to the second and last jarful. Whereupon he attempted to get up and after a little time suc-ceeded. He looked very severe.

The other Elders concurred, with frowning glances at those around them.

'But you can't take that away!' shouted the Bard who, when not making poetry, was given to irreverence. 'I haven't had one yet!'

16

'You'll go without, then,' said the Elder.

'I'm damned if I will!'

'You'll be damned anyway,' said the Elder, whose eyes now had a piercing and terrible power. 'And moreover, if you speak again I'll report you to the Druid and have you up before the Session.' The vehemence in so old a man was astonishing.

'Report away!' shouted the Bard in a right fury.

The Elders began moving away with the evidence. The Bard swung round upon the others to incite them, but the Discoverer, catching his eye, winked slowly, and presently said to him in a low voice, 'I smuggled a jar round the corner.'

Looking after the Elders and noting their solemn if uncertain gait, the Bard broke into loud laughter. In a little while his companions were all dissolved in this laughter.

'You weren't very civil to him, all the same. What'll you say if we're had up?'

But the Bard was now on the crest of creation and finished his improvisation with a roar:

'... civil?
With usquebea we'll face the devil!'

Druids and chiefs, clans and federated clans, became the sport of their thought, the playthings of their wit.

But on the Seventh Day, the Druid preached from the text, 'The water of life – *and of death*', and divided his discourse under many heads. It was a cogent exhaustive piece of work, within the subtle pattern of which there began to glimmer an eldritch fire, a loch of fire growing big as a sea, convoluting and molten and tinct of brimstone. Certain of the listeners felt themselves fall in and sink – and sink – and sink ... 'yet though you keep on sinking to all eternity you will never reach the bottom.'

On the way home, the Bard tried to persuade the Discoverer to go to the hill stream, but the Discoverer would not go with him.

'Frightened?' said the Bard. 'Humph! But I wonder how he knew so much about it?'

'It's his business to think Hell out,' said the Discoverer simply.

'Hell? Who's talking of Hell? I mean, how did he know so much about uisgebeatha? *Who drank the Elders' jar?*'

The Discoverer stopped dead, and on his face appeared evidence of the eternal dichotomy in the spirit of his tribe: wonder and fear, reverence and unholiness, wild laughter in an awful hush, saint and demon. He would put in authority those whom he would take down. For he was branded by the One God with the awful brand of the undying individualist.

'It's all right,' said the Bard. 'They would never suspect us so soon after the sermon.' And as they went on their way he added thoughtfully, 'This is a new thing and we'll have to think it out for ourselves.'

And it seems he was right, for his tribe are still making the usquebeatha, and still thinking it out – nearly as violently as ever.

Whisky and Scotland

Robert Burns

Freedom and Whisky Gang Thegither

These stanzas form the concluding part of a poem addressed by Burns to the Scottish Members of Parliament urging them to play their part in reforming the Wash Act of 1784 which was intended to control whisky distilling in Scotland after complaints by English distillers of gin that the Scots were more favourably treated. The Wash Act, with its new powers given to excisemen, was immensely unpopular in Scotland. It was replaced by the more acceptable Scotch Distillery Act of 1786, much to Burns's satisfaction.

Let half-starv'd slaves in warmer skies
See future wines, rich-clust'ring, rise;
Their lot auld Scotland ne'er envies,
   But blyth an' frisky,
She eyes her freeborn, martial boys,
   Tak aff their Whisky.

What tho' their Phebus kinder warms,
While Fragrance blooms and Beauty charms!
When wretches range, in famish'd swarms,
    The scented groves,
Or hounded forth, dishonor arms,
    In hungry droves.

Their gun's a burden on their shouther;
They downa bide the stink o' powther;
Their bauldest thought's a hank'ring swither,
    To stan' or rin,
Till skelp – a shot – they're aff, a' throu'ther,
    To save their skin.

But bring a Scotchman frae his hill,
Clap in his cheek a highlan gill,
Say, such is royal George's will,
    An' there's the foe,
He has nae thought but how to kill
    Twa at a blow.

Nae cauld, faint-hearted doubtings tease him;
Daeth comes, with fearless eye he sees him;
Wi' bluidy hand a welcome gies him;
    An' when he fa's,
His latest draught o' breathin lea'es him
    In faint huzzas.

Sages their solemn een may steek,
An' raise a philosophic reek,
And physically causes seek,
    In clime an' season,
But tell me Whisky's name in Greek,
    I'll tell the reason.

Scotland, my auld, respected Mither!
Tho' whiles ye moistify your leather,
Till whare ye sit, on craps o' heather,
    Ye tine your dam;
Freedom and Whisky gang thegither,
    Tak aff your dram!

The Author's Earnest Cry and Prayer (Postscript)

Christopher North

The Real Glenlivet

John Wilson (1785–1854), who wrote under the pen-name of Christopher North, was the principal author of a series of invented conversations, conducted by real people under assumed names, that appeared in *Blackwood's Magazine* between 1822 and 1835 under the title *Noctes Ambrosianae* (Ambrosian Nights): Ambrose's was the name of the Edinburgh tavern where the conversations took place, in a highly convivial atmosphere. This sentiment about the virtues of Glenlivet, the classic pot-still malt whisky, is put into the mouth of the poet James Hogg, whom Wilson called the Ettrick Shepherd, as Hogg really had begun life as a shepherd and was widely regarded as a self-taught rustic genius. Wilson built up his character in the *Noctes* with condescending affection as a loquacious, sentimental, heavy-drinking, romantic lover of nature.

North. The jug is a most excellent one, James. Edinburgh is supplied with very fine water.

Shepherd. Gie me the real Glenleevit – such as Awmrose aye has in the hoose – and I weel believe that I could mak drinkable toddy out o' seawater. The human mind never tires o' Glenleevit, ony mair than o' cauler air. If a body could just find out the exac proper proportion o' quantity that ought to be drank every day, and keep to that, I verily trow that he micht leeve for ever, without dying at a', and that doctors and kirkyards would go out of fashion.

Noctes Ambrosianae

Elizabeth Grant of Rothiemurchus

A Highland Lady Remembers

Elizabeth Grant (1797–1885) was the daughter of a lawyer and
Highland landowner; her posthumously published memoirs are an
important source for our knowledge of social life both in the Highlands and in Edinburgh in the first part of the nineteenth century.

The Dell was an ugly place, a small low house, only two or three stunted
trees in the garden behind it, and a wide, sandy, stony plane all round,
never a bit the more fertile for the regular inundation at the Lammas
tide when the Druie always overflowed its banks. Here the first lairds of
Rothiemurchus had lived after a fashion that must have been of the
simplest. It then became the jointure house, and in it the Lady Jean
passed her widowhood with a few fields and £100 a year. Mrs Macintosh
was a tidy guid-wife, but nothing beyond the thriving farmer's helpmate.
She and her husband lived mostly in the kitchen, and each in their own
department did the work of a head servant. The cheer she offered us was
never more than bread and cheese and whisky, but the oaten bread was
so fresh and crisp, the butter so delicious, and the cheese – not the
ordinary skimmed milk curd, the leavings of the dairy, but the Saturday's
kebbuck made of the overnight and the morning's milk, poured cream
and all into the yearnin tub; the whisky was a bad habit, there was
certainly too much of it going. At every house it was offered, at every
house it must be tasted or offence would be given, so we were taught to
believe. I am sure now that had we steadily refused compliance with so
incorrect a custom it would have been far better for ourselves, and might
all the more sooner have put a stop to so pernicious a habit among the
people. Whisky-drinking was and is the bane of that country; from early
morning till late at night it went on. Decent gentle-women began the
day with a dram. In our house the bottle of whisky, with its accompaniment of a silver salver full of small glasses, was placed on the side-table
with cold meat every morning. In the pantry a bottle of whisky was the
allowance per day, with bread and cheese in any required quantity, for
such messengers or visitors whose errands sent them in that direction.
The very poorest cottages could offer whisky; all the men engaged in the
wood manufacture drank it in goblets three times a day, yet except at a
merry-making we never saw any one tipsy. . . .

The next incident that comes back on memory is the death of old George Ross, the hen-wife's husband; he caught cold, and inflammation came on; a bottle of whisky, or maybe more, failed to cure him, so he died, and was waked, after the old fashion, shaved and partly dressed and set up in his bed, all the country-side collecting round him. After abundance of refreshment the company set to dancing, when, from the jolting of the floor, out tumbled the corpse into the midst of the reel, and away scampered the guests screaming and declaring the old man had come to life again. As the bereaved wife had not been the gentlest of helpmates, this was supposed to be 'a warning' – of what was not declared; all that was plain was that the spirit of the deceased was dissatisfied; many extraordinary signs were spoken of, as we heard from my mother's maid. . . .

The Spey floaters lived mostly down near Ballindalloch, a certain number of families by whom the calling had been followed for ages, to whom the wild river, all its holes and shoals and rocks and shiftings, were as well known as had its bed been dry. They came up in the season, at the first hint of a *spate*, as a rise in the water was called. A large bothy was built for them at the mouth of the Druie in a fashion that suited themselves; a fire on a stone hearth in the middle of the floor, a hole in the very centre of the roof just over it where some of the smoke got out, heather spread on the ground, no window, and there, after their hard day's work, they lay down for the night, in their wet clothes – for they had been perhaps hours in the river – each man's feet to the fire, each man's plaid round his chest, a circle of wearied bodies half stupefied by whisky, enveloped in a cloud of steam and smoke, and sleeping soundly till the morning. They were a healthy race, suffering little except in their old age from rheumatism. They made their large rafts themselves, seldom taking help from our woodmen, yet often giving it if there were an over-quantity of timber in the runs.

Mr Macintosh, who often dined at the Doune, usually contrived to come the day before a log-run, our particular delight, so we were sure of appearing in the very height of the business before the noontide rest. When the men met in the morning they were supposed to have break-fasted at home, and perhaps had had their private dram, it being cold work in a dark wintry dawn, to start over the moor for a walk of some miles to end in standing up to the knees in water; yet on collecting, whisky was always handed round; a lad with a small cask – a quarter anker – on his back, and a horn cup in his hand that held a gill, appeared three times a day among them. They all took their 'morning' raw, undiluted and without accompaniment, so they did the gill at parting when the work was done; but the noontide dram was part of a meal. There was a twenty minutes' rest from labour, and a bannock and a bit of

24

cheese taken out of every pocket to be eaten leisurely with the whisky. when we were there the horn cup was offered first to us, and each of us took a sip to the health of our friends around us, who all stood up. Sometimes a floater's wife or bairn would come with a message; such messenger was always offered whisky. Aunt Mary had a story that one day a woman with a child in her arms, and another bit thing at her knee, came up among them; the horn cup was duly handed to her, she took a 'gey guid drap' herself, and then gave a little to each of the babies. 'My goodness, child,' said my mother to the wee thing that was trotting by the mother's side, 'doesn't it *bite* you?' 'Ay, but I like the bite,' replied the creature.

Memoirs of a Highland Lady

Robert Fergusson

The Daft-Days

Robert Fergusson (1750–74), the Edinburgh poet so admired by Burns, died in the city's public Bedlam at a tragically early age. Here he celebrates the festivities that went on during the 'Daft-Days', the period between Christmas and Handsel Monday (the first Monday of the year). 'Auld Reikie' (old Smokey) is Edinburgh; 'Tulloch Gorum' was a popular drinking song.

Now mirk December's dowie face
    Glours our the rigs wi' sour grimace,
While, thro' his *minimum* of space,
    The bleer-ey'd sun,
Wi' blinkin light and stealing pace,
    His race doth run.

From naked groves nae birdie sings,
To shepherd's pipe nae hillock rings,
The breeze nae od'rous flavour brings
    From *Borean* cave,
And dwyning nature droops her wings,
    Wi' visage grave.

Mankind but scanty pleasure glean
Frae snawy hill or barren plain,
Whan Winter, 'midst his nipping train,
    Wi' frozen spear,
Sends drift owr a' his bleak domain,
    And guides the weir.

Auld Reikie! thou'rt the canty hole,
A bield for mony caldrife soul,
Wha snugly at thine ingle loll,
    Baith warm and couth;
While round they gar the bicker roll
    To weet their mouth.

When merry Yule-day comes, I trow
You'll scantlins find a hungry mou;
Sma' are our cares, our stamacks fou
    O' gusty gear,
And kickshaws, strangers to our view,
    Sin Fairn-year.

Ye browster wives, now busk ye bra,
And fling your sorrows far awa';
Then come and gies the tither blaw
    Of reaming ale,
Mair precious than the well of *Spa*,
    Our hearts to heal.

Then, tho' at odds wi' a' the warl'
Amang oursells we'll never quarrel;
Tho' Discord gie a canker'd snarl
    To spoil our glee,
As lang's there's pith into the barrel
    We'll drink and 'gree.

Fidlers, your pins in temper fix,
And roset weel your fiddle-sticks,
And banish vile Italian tricks
    From out your quorum,
Nor *fortes* wi' *pianos* mix,
    Gie's *Tulloch Gorum*.

For nought can cheer the heart sae weil
As can a canty Highland reel,
It even vivifies the heel
    To skip and dance:
Lifeless is he wha canna feel
    Its influence.

Let mirth abound, let social cheer
Invest the dawning of the year;
Let blithesome innocence appear
    To crown our joy,
Nor envy wi' sarcastic sneer
    Our bliss destroy.

And thou, great god of *Aqua Vitae!*
Wha sways the empire of this city,
When fou we're sometimes capernoity,
    Be thou prepar'd
To hedge us frae that black banditti,
    The City-Guard.

David Macbeth Moir

Benjie's Christening

David Macbeth Moir (1798–1851) was an editor of *Blackwood's Magazine* in whose pages the source of this extract, *The Life of Mansie Wauch*, first appeared as a serial from 1824 onwards: it was published in book form in 1828. In its affectionate presentation of life in a small Lowland Scottish town, full of 'humours' and senti-mentalities and dialogue in Scots, it helped to establish the tradition of Scottish rural manners that was later developed by the 'Kailyard' school of Scottish fiction.

At the christening of our only bairn, Benjie, two or three remarkable circumstances occurred, which it behoves me to relate.

It was on a cold November afternoon; and really when the bit room was all redd up, the fire bleezing away, and the candles lighted, every thing looked full tosh and comfortable. It was a real pleasure, after looking out into the drift that was fleeing like mad from the east, to turn one's neb inwards, and think that we had a civilized home to comfort us in the dreary season. So, one after another, the bit party we had invited to the ceremony came papping in; and the crack began to get loud and hearty; for, to speak the truth, we were blessed with canny friends, and a good neighbourhood. Notwithstanding, it was very curious, that I had no mind of asking down James Batter, the weaver, honest man, though he was one of our own elders; and in papped James, just when the company had haffins met, with his stocking-sleeves on his arms, his nightcap on his head; and his blue-stained apron hanging down before him, to light his pipe at our fire.

James, when he saw his mistake, was fain to make his retreat; but we would not hear tell of it, till he came in, and took a dram out of the bottle, as we told him the not doing so would spoil the wean's beauty, which is an old freak, (the small-pox, however, afterwards did that;) so, with much persuasion, he took a chair for a gliff, and began with some of his drolls – for he is a clever, humoursome man, as ye ever met with. But he had now got far on with his jests, when lo! a rap came to the door, and Mysie whipped away the bottle under her apron, saying, 'Wheesht, wheesht, for the sake of gudeness, there's the minister!'

29

The room had only one door, and James mistook it, running his head, for lack of knowledge, into the open closet, just as the minister lifted the outer-door sneck. We were all now sitting on nettles, for we were frighted that James would be seized with a cough, for he was a wee asthmatic; or that some, knowing there was a thief in the pantry, might hurt good manners by breaking out into a giggle. However, all for a considerable time was quiet, and the ceremony was performed; little Nancy, our niece, handing the bairn upon my arm to receive its name. So, we thought, as the minister seldom made a long stay on similar occasions, that all would pass off well enough – But wait a wee.

There was but one of our company that had not cast up, to wit, Deacon Paunch, the flesher, a most worthy man, but tremendously big, and grown to the very heels; as was once seen on a wager, that his ankle was greater than my brans. It was really a pain to all feeling Christians, to see the worthy man waigling about, being, when weighed in his own scales, two-and-twenty stone ten ounces, Dutch weight. Honest man, he had had a sore fecht with the wind and the sleet, and he came in with a shawl roppined round his neck, peching like a broken-winded horse; so fain was he to find a rest for his weary carcass in our stuffed chintz pattern elbow-chair by the fire cheek.

From the soughing of wind at the window, and the rattling in the lum, it was clear to all manner of comprehension, that the night was a dismal one; so the minister, seeing so many of his own douce folk about him, thought he might do worse than volunteer to sit still, and try our toddy: indeed, we would have pressed him before this to do so; but what was to come of James Batter, who was shut up in the closet, like the spies in the house of Rahab, the harlot, in the city of Jericho?

James began to find it was a bad business; and having been driving the shuttle about from before daylight, he was fain to cruik his hough, and felt round about him quietly in the dark for a chair to sit down upon, since better might not be. But, wae's me! the cat was soon out of the pock.

Me and the minister were just argle-bargling some few words on the doctrine of the camel and the eye of the needle, when, in the midst of our discourse, as all was wheesht and attentive, an awful thud was heard in the closet, which gave the minister, who thought the house had fallen down, such a start, that his very wig louped for a full three-eighths off his crown. I say we were needcessitated to let the cat out of the pock for two reasons; firstly, because we did not know what had happened; and, secondly, to quiet the minister's fears, decent man, for he was a wee nervous. So we made a hearty laugh of it, as well as we could, and opened the door to bid James Batter come out, as we confessed all. Easier said than done, howsoever. When we pulled open the door, and took forward one of the candles, there was James doubled up, sticking two-fold like a rotten in a sneck-trap, in an old chair, the bottom of which had gone down before him, and which, for some craize about it, had been put out of the way by Nanse, that no accident might happen. Save us! if the deacon had sate down upon it, pity on our brick-floor.

Well, after some ado, we got James, who was more frighted than hurt, hauled out of his hidy-hole; and after lifting of his cowl, and sleeking down his front hair, he took a seat beside us, apologeezing for not being in his Sunday's garb, the which the minister, who was a free and easy man, declared there was no occasion for, and begged him to make himself comfortable.

Well, passing over that business, Mr Wiggie and me entered into our humours, for the drappikie was beginning to tell on my noddle, and make me somewhat venturesome – not to say that I was not a little proud to have the minister in my bit housie; so, says I to him in a cosh way, 'Ye may believe me or no, Mr Wiggie, but mair than me think ye out of sight the best preacher in the parish – nane of them, Mr Wiggie, can hold the candle to ye, man.'

'Weesht, weesht,' said the body, in rather a cold way that I did not expect, knowing him to be as proud as a peacock – 'I daresay I am just like my neighbours.'

This was not quite so kind – so says I to him, 'Maybe, sae, for many a one thinks ye could not hold a candle to Mr Blowster the Cameronian, that whiles preaches at Lugton.'

This was a stramp on his corny toe. 'Na, na,' answered Mr Wiggie, rather nettled; 'let us drop that subject. I preach like my neighbours. Some of them may be worse, and others better; just as some of your own trade may make clothes worse, and some better, than yourself.'

My corruption was raised. 'I deny that,' said I, in a brisk manner, which I was sorry for after – 'I deny that, Mr Wiggie,' says I to him; 'I'll make a pair of breeches with the face of clay.'

But this was only a passing breeze, during the which, howsoever, I happened to swallow my thimble, which accidentally slipped off my middle finger, causing both me and the company general alarm, as there were great fears that it might mortify in the stomach; but it did not; and neither word nor wittens of it have been seen or heard tell of from that to this day. So, in two or three minutes, we had some few good songs, and a round of Scotch proverbs, when the clock chapped eleven. We were all getting, I must confess, a thought noisy; Johnny Soutter having broken a dram-glass, and Willie Fegs couped a bottle on the bit table-cloth; all noisy, I say, except Deacon Paunch, douce man, who had fallen into a pleasant slumber; so, when the minister rose to take his hat, they all rose except the Deacon, whom we shook by the arms for some time, but in vain, to waken him. His round, oily face, good creature, was just as if it had been cut out of a big turnip, it was so fat, fozy, and soft; but at last, after some ado, we succeeded, and he looked about him with a wild stare, opening his two red eyes, like Pandore oysters, asking what had

31

happened; and we got him hoized up on his legs, tying the blue shawl round his bull-neck again.

Our company had not got well out of the door, and I was priding myself in my heart, about being landlord to such a goodly turn out, when Nanse took me by the arm, and said, 'Come, and see such an unearthly sight.' This startled me, and I hesitated; but, at long and last, I went in with her, a thought alarmed at what had happened, and – my gracious!! there on the easy-chair, was our bonny tortoise-shell cat, Tommy, with the red morocco collar about its neck, bruised as flat as a flounder, and as dead as a mawk!!!

The Deacon had sat down upon it without thinking; and the poor animal, that our neighbours' bairns used to play with, and be so fond of, was crushed out of life without a cheep. The thing, doubtless, was not intended, but it gave Nanse and me a very sore heart.

The Life of Mansie Wauch

Edward Burt

Scots Drinkers versus English

Edward Burt (*d.* 1755) was employed by General Wade when he was building military roads in Scotland in the 1720s. His *Letters*, from which this extract comes, did not appear until 1754. Burt's shrewd and humorous observations present a vivid picture of aspects of social and cultural life of Scotland in the early eighteenth century.

Some of the Highland Gentlemen are immoderate Drinkers of Usky, even three or four Quarts at a Sitting; and in general, the People that can pay the Purchase, drink it without Moderation.

Not long ago, four *English* Officers took a Fancy to try their Strength in this Bow of *Ulysses*, against a like Number of the Country Champions, but the Enemy came off victorious; and one of the Officers was thrown into a Fit of the Gout, without Hopes; another had a most dangerous Fever, a third lost his Skin and Hair by the Surfeit, and the last confessed to me, that when Drunkenness and Debate run high, he took several Opportunities to sham it.

They say for Excuse, the Country requires a great deal; but I think they mistake a Habit and Custom for Necessity. They likewise pretend it does not intoxicate in the Hills as it would do in the low Country, but this also I doubt by their own Practice; for those among them who have any Consideration will hardly care so much as to refresh themselves with it, when they pass near the Tops of the Mountains; for in that Circumstance, they say, it renders them careless, listless of the Fatigue, and inclined to sit down, which might invite to Sleep, and then they would be in Danger to perish with Cold. I have been tempted to think this Spirit has in it, by Infusion, the Seeds of Anger, Revenge and Murder (this I confess is a little too poetical) but those who drink of it to any Degree of Excess behave, for the most Part, like true Barbarians, I think much beyond the Effect of other Liquors. The Collector of the Customs at *Stornway* in the Isle of *Lewis* told me, that about 120 Families drink yearly 4000 *English* Gallons of this Spirit, and Brandy together, although many of them are so poor they cannot afford to pay for much of either, which you know must increase the Quantity drank by the rest, and that they frequently give to Children of six or seven Years old, as much at a time as an ordinary Wine-glass will hold.

When they chuse to qualify it for Punch they sometimes mix it with Water and Honey, or with Milk and Honey; at other times the Mixture is only the *Aqua Vitae*, Sugar and Butter, this they burn till the Butter and Sugar are dissolved.

Letters from a Gentleman in the North of Scotland

Robert Burns

Willie Brew'd a Peck o' Maut

This frank celebration of drunkenness derives from a real event.
'Willie' was William Nicol, master at the High School in Edinburgh, with whom Burns (1759−96) formed a close friendship
when he visited the city in 1786−7; Rob was Burns himself. Allan
was Allan Masterton, who composed the air to which Burns wrote
these words.

O Willie brew'd a peck o' maut,
    And Rob and Allan cam to see;
Three blyther hearts, the lee lang night,
    Ye wadna found in Christendie.

Chorus

We are na fou, we're nae that fou,
    But just a drappie in our e'e;
The cock may craw, the day may daw,
    And ay we'll taste the barley bree.

Here are we met, three merry boys,
    Three merry boys I trow are we;
And mony a night we've merry been,
    And mony mae we hope to be!

Chorus, We are na fou, &c.

Is that the moon, I ken her horn,
    That's blinkin in the lift sae hie;
She shines sae bright to wyle us hame,
    But by my sooth she'll wait a wee!

Chorus, We are na fou, &c.

Wha first shall rise to gang awa'
    A cuckold, coward loon is he!
Wha first beside his chair shall fa',
    He is the king amang us three.

Chorus, We are na fou, &c.

Dean Ramsay

Drinking Prowess

Edward Ramsay (1793–1872) was born in Aberdeen, educated in
England, and in 1824 settled in Edinburgh as assistant to the
Bishop of Edinburgh (in the Scottish Episcopal Church), becoming
dean in 1841. From then until his death he was, as 'Dean Ramsay',
a well-known and much loved Edinburgh worthy, with friends
among all religious denominations.

In my part of the country the traditionary stories of drinking prowess are
quite marvellous. On Deeside there flourished a certain Saunders Paul
(whom I remember an old man), an innkeeper at Banchory. He was said
to have drunk whisky, glass for glass, to the claret of Mr Maule and the
Laird of Skene for a whole evening; and in those days there was a
traditional story of his despatching, at one sitting, in company with a
character celebrated for conviviality – one of the men employed to float
rafts of timber down the Dee – three dozen of porter. Of this Mr Paul it
was recorded that, on being asked if he considered porter as a whole-
some beverage, he replied, 'Oh yes, if you don't take above a dozen.'
Saunders Paul was, as I have said, the innkeeper at Banchory; his friend
and *porter* companion was drowned in the Dee, and when told that the
body had been found down the stream below Crathes, he coolly remarked, 'I am surprised at that, for I never kenn'd him pass the inn
before without comin' in for a glass.'

Some relatives of mine travelling in the Highlands were amused by
observing in a small roadside public-house a party drinking, whose ap-
paratus for conviviality called forth the dry, quaint humour which is so
thoroughly Scottish. These drovers had met together and were celebrating their meeting by a liberal consumption of whisky; the inn could only
furnish one glass without a bottom, and this the party passed on from
one to another. A queer-looking, pawky chield, whenever the glass came
to his turn, remarked most gravely, 'I think we wadna be the waur o'
some water,' taking care, however, never to add any of the simple
element, but quietly drank off his glass.

There was a sort of infatuation in the supposed dignity and manliness
attached to powers of deep potation, and the fatal effects of drinking
were spoken of in a manner both reckless and unfeeling. Thus, I have

been assured that a well-known old laird of the old school expressed himself with great indignation at the charge brought against hard drinking that it had actually *killed* people. 'Na na, I never knew onybody killed wi' drinking, but I hae ken'd some that dee'd in the training.' . . .

There was a sort of dogged tone of apology for excess in drinking which marked the hold which the practice had gained on ordinary minds. Of this we have a remarkable example in the unwilling testimony of a witness who was examined as to the fact of drunkenness being charged against a minister. The person examined was beadle or one of the church officials. He was asked, 'Did you ever see the minister the worse of drink?' 'I canna say I've seen him the waur o' drink, but nae doubt I've seen him the *better* o't,' was the evasive answer. The question, however, was pushed further; and when he was urged to say if this state of being 'the better for drink' ever extended to a condition of absolute helpless intoxication, the reply was: 'Indeed, afore that cam' I was blind fou mysel', and I could see naething.' . . .

. . . I am assured of the truth of the following anecdote by a son of the gentleman who acted as chief mourner on the occasion: About seventy years ago, an old maiden lady died in Strathspey. Just previous to her death, she sent for her grand-nephew, and said to him, 'Willy, I'm deein', and as ye'll hae the charge o' a' I have, mind now that as much whisky is to be used at my funeral as there was at my baptism.' Willy neglected to ask the old lady what the quantity of whisky used at the baptism was, but when the day of the funeral arrived, believed her orders would be best fulfilled by allowing each guest to drink as much as he pleased. The churchyard where the body was to be deposited was about ten miles distant from where the death occurred. It was a short day in November, and when the funeral party came to the churchyard, the shades of night had considerably closed in. The grave-digger, whose patience had been exhausted in waiting, was not in the least willing to accept of Captin G————'s (the chief mourner) apology for delay. After looking about him, he put the anxious question, 'But, Captain, whaur's Miss Ketty?' The reply was: 'In her coffin, to be sure, and get it into the earth as fast as you can.' There, however, was no coffin; the procession had sojourned at a country inn by the way, had rested the body on a dyke, started without it, and had to postpone the interment until next day....

Reminiscences of Scottish Life and Character

Edward Topham

In an Oyster Cellar

Edward Topham (1751–1820) was an English journalist, play-wright and traveller as well as a captain in the Life Guards. This is one of his *Letters From Edinburgh*, which appeared in 1776. They are an important source for our knowledge of social life in Edin-burgh in the eighteenth century. Topham's lively style and acute powers of observation make the book a pleasure to read.

Edinburgh, January 15, 1775.

Sir,

You have so frequently run the round of all the fashionable diversions in other countries, as well as your own, and have so long imagined that gilded roofs and painted ceilings are the only scenes of festivity, that you will not easily believe there exist any other. There is, however, a species of entertainment, different indeed from yours, but which seems to give more real pleasure to the company who visit it, than either Ranelagh or the Pantheon. The votaries to this shrine of pleasure are numerous, and the manner is intirely new. As soon as the evening begins to grow late, a large party form themselves together, and march to the Temple where, after descending a few steps for the benefit of being removed from profaner eyes, they are admitted by the good Guardian of it; who, doubtless, rejoices to see so large and well-disposed a company of wor-shippers. The Temple itself is very plain and humble. It knows no idle ornaments, no sculpture or painting, nor even so much as wax tapers – a few solitary candles of tallow cast a dim, religious light, very well adapted to the scene. There are many separate cells of different sizes, accommo-dated to the number of the religious, who attend in greater or smaller parties, as the spirit moves them. After the company have made the proper sacrifices, and staid as long as they think necessary, the utensils are removed, proper donations made to the priestess; who, like all others of her profession, is not very averse to money, and they retire in good order, and disperse for the evening.

In plain terms, this shrine of festivity is nothing more than an Oyster-cellar, and its Votaries the First People in Edinburgh. A few evenings

ago I had the pleasure of being asked to one of these entertainments, by a Lady. At that time I was not acquainted with this scene of 'high life below stairs,' and therefore, when she mentioned the word Oyster Cellar, I imagined I must have mistaken the place of invitation: she repeated it, however, and I found it was not my business to make objections; so agreed immediately. You will not think it very odd, that I should expect, from the place where the appointment was made, to have had a *partie tête-à-tête*. I thought I was bound in honour to keep it a secret, and waited with great impatience till the hour arrived. When the clock struck the hour fixed on, away I went, and enquired if the lady was there – 'O yes,' cried the woman, 'she has been here an hour or more.' I had just time to curse my want of punctuality, when the door opened, and I had

41

the pleasure of being ushered in, not to one lady, as I expected, but to a large and brilliant company of both sexes, most of whom I had the honour of being acquainted with.

The large table, round which they were seated, was covered with dishes full of oysters, and pots of porter. For a long time, I could not suppose that this was the only entertainment we were to have, and I sat waiting in expectation of a repast that was never to make its appearance. This I soon found verified, as the table was cleared, and glasses introduced. The ladies were now asked whether they would choose brandy or rum punch? I thought this question an odd one, but I was soon informed by the gentleman who sat next me, that no wine was sold here; but that punch was quite 'the thing'. The ladies, who always love what is best, fixed upon brandy punch, and a large bowl was immediately introduced. The conversation hitherto had been insipid, and at intervals it now became general and lively. The women, who, to do them justice, are much more entertaining than their neighbours in England, discovered a great deal of vivacity and fondness for repartee. A thousand things were hazarded, and met with applause; to which the oddity of the scene gave propriety, and which could have been produced in no other place. The general ease, with which they conducted themselves, the innocent freedom of their manners, and their unaffected good-nature, all conspired to make us forget that we were regaling in a cellar; and was a convincing proof, that, let local customs operate as they may, a truly polite woman is every where the same. Bigotted as I know you to be to more fashionable amusements, you yourself would have confessed, that there was in this little assembly more real happiness and mirth, than in all the ceremonious and splendid meetings at Soho.

Letters from Edinburgh

Anonymous

The Ballad of Kind Kyttok

This poem was once attributed to the great Middle Scots poet
William Dunbar, but it is not now thought to be by him, and its
author remains unknown.

My gude dame was a gay wife, bot she was richt gend,
She dwelt furth far into France, upon Falkland Fell;
Thay callit her Kind Kyttok, wha sa her weill kend.
She was like a cauldron cruke clear under kell;
They threpit that she deit of thirst, and made a gude end.
Efter her deid, she dreadit nocht in heaven for to dwell;
And sa to heaven the hieway dreidless she wend,
      Yet she wanderit and yede by to an elriche well.
      She met there, as I ween,
      An ask ridand on a snail,
      And cryit, 'Ourtane fallow, hail!'
      And rade an inch behind the tail,
      Till it was near e'en.

Sa she had hap to be horsit to her herbry,
At an alehouse near heaven it nightit them there;
She deit of thirst in this warld, that gert her be sa dry,
She never eat, bot drank our measure and mair.
She sleepit till the morn at noon, and rais airly;
And to the yetts of heaven fast can the wif fare;
And by Saint Peter, in at the yett she stall privily;
God lukit and saw her lettin in, and lewch his hairt sair.
      And there, yearis seven
      She livit a gude life,
      And was our Ladyis hen-wife:
      And held Saint Peter at strife,
      Ay, while she was in heaven.

She lookit out on a day, and thocht right lang
To see the alehouse beside, intil an evil hour;
And out of heaven the high gait cowth the wife gang
For to get her ane fresh drink, the ale of heaven was sour.
She come again to heavenis yett, when the bell rang,
Saint Peter hit her with a club, till a great clour
Rais in her heid, because the wif yede wrang.
Than to the alehouse again she ran, the pitcheris to pour,
 And for to brew and bake.
 Friends I pray you hertfully,
 Gif ye be thirsty or dry,
 Drink with my guddame, as ye gae by,
 Anis for my sake.

Sir Walter Scott

High Jinks in Edinburgh

This picture of an eighteenth-century Edinburgh lawyer relaxing with a childish game of make-believe shows Scott's passionate interest in social manners and customs in the generations immediately preceding his own (he was born in 1771). Scott was himself a lawyer and the son of a lawyer, and was intimately acquainted with the customs and traditions of Scottish men of law.

Dinmont descended confidently, then turned into a dark alley – then up a dark stair – and then into an open door. While he was whistling shrilly for the waiter as if he had been one of his collie dogs, Mannering looked round him, and could hardly conceive how a gentleman of a liberal profession, and good society, should choose such a scene for social indulgence. Besides the miserable entrance, the house itself seemed paltry and half ruinous. The passage in which they stood had a window to the close, which admitted a little light during the day-time, and a villainous compound of smells at all times, but more especially towards evening. Corresponding to this window was a borrowed light on the other side of the passage, looking into the kitchen, which had no direct communication with the free air, but received in the daytime, at second hand, such straggling and obscure light as found its way from the lane through the window opposite. At present, the interior of the kitchen was visible by its own huge fires – a sort of Pandemonium, where men and women, half undressed, were busied in baking, broiling, roasting oysters, and preparing devils on the gridiron; the mistress of the place, with her shoes slipshod, and her hair straggling like that of Megæra from under a round-eared cap, toiling, scolding, receiving orders, giving them, and obeying them all at once, seemed the presiding enchantress of that gloomy and fiery region.

Loud and repeated bursts of laughter, from different quarters of the house, proved that her labours were acceptable, and not unrewarded by a generous public. With some difficulty a waiter was prevailed upon to show Colonel Mannering and Dinmont the room where their friend, learned in the law, held his hebdomadal carousals. The scene which it exhibited, and particularly the attitude of the counsellor himself, the principal figure therein, struck his two clients with amazement.

45

Mr Pleydell was a lively, sharp-looking gentleman, with a professional shrewdness in his eye, and, generally speaking, a professional formality in his manners. But this, like his three-tailed wig and black coat, he could slip off on a Saturday evening, when surrounded by a party of jolly companions, and disposed for what he called his altitudes. On the present occasion, the revel had lasted since four o'clock, and, at length, under the direction of a venerable compotator, who had shared the sports and festivity of three generations, the frolicsome company had begun to practise the ancient and now forgotten pastime of *High Jinks*. This game was played in several different ways. Most frequently the dice were thrown by the company, and those upon whom the lot fell were obliged to assume and maintain, for a time, a certain fictitious character, or to repeat a certain number of fescennine verses in a particular order. If they departed from the characters assigned, or if their memory proved treacherous in the repetition, they incurred forfeits, which were either compounded for by swallowing an additional bumper, or by paying a small sum towards the reckoning. At this sport the jovial company were closely engaged, when Mannering entered the room.

Mr Counsellor Pleydell, such as we have described him, was enthroned, as a monarch, in an elbow-chair, placed on the dining-table, his scratch wig on one side, his head crowned with a bottle-slider, his eye leering with an expression betwixt fun and the effects of wine, while his court around him resounded with such crambo scraps of verse as these:

> Where is Gerunto now? and what's become of him?
> Gerunto's drowned because he could not swim, &c., &c.

Such, O Themis, were anciently the sports of thy Scottish children! Dinmont was first in the room. He stood aghast a moment, – and then exclaimed, 'It's him, sure enough – Deil o' the like o' that ever I saw!'

At the sound of 'Mr Dinmont and Colonel Mannering wanting to speak to you, sir,' Pleydell turned his head, and blushed a little when he saw the very genteel figure of the English stranger. He was, however, of the opinion of Falstaff, 'Out, ye villains, play out the play!' wisely judging it the better way to appear totally unconcerned. 'Where be our guards?' exclaimed this second Justinian: 'see ye not a stranger knight from foreign parts arrived at this our court of Holyrood, – with our bold yeoman Andrew Dinmont, who has succeeded to the keeping of our royal flocks within the forest of Jedwood, where, thanks to our royal care in the administration of justice, they feed as safe as if they were within the bounds of Fife? Where be our heralds, our pursuivants, our Lyon, our Marchmount, our Carrick, and our Snowdown? Let the strangers be placed at our board and regaled as beseemeth their quality, and this our high holiday – to-morrow we will hear their tidings.'

'So please you, my liege, to-morrow's Sunday,' said one of the company.

'Sunday, is it? then we will give no offence to the assembly of the kirk – on Monday shall be their audience.'

Mannering, who had stood at first uncertain whether to advance or retreat, now resolved to enter for the moment into the whim of the scene, though internally fretting at Mac-Morlan, for sending him to consult with a crack-brained humourist. He therefore advanced with three profound congees, and craved permission to lay his credentials at the feet of the Scottish monarch, in order to be perused at his best leisure. The gravity with which he accommodated himself to the humour of the moment, and the deep and humble inclination with which he at first declined, and then accepted, a seat presented by the master of the ceremonies, procured him three rounds of applause.

'Deil hae me, if they arena a' mad thegither!' said Dinmont, occupying with less ceremony a seat at the bottom of the table, 'or else they hae taen Yule before it comes, and are gaun a-guisarding.'

A large glass of claret was offered to Mannering, who drank it to the health of the reigning prince. 'You are, I presume to guess,' said the monarch, 'that celebrated Sir Miles Mannering, so renowned in the French wars, and may well pronounce to us if the wines of Gascony lose their flavour in our more northern realm.'

Mannering, agreeably flattered by this allusion to the fame of his celebrated ancestor, replied, by professing himself only a distant relation of the preux chevalier, and added, 'that in his opinion the wine was superlatively good.'

'It's ower cauld for my stamach,' said Dinmont, setting down the glass (empty, however).

'We will correct that quality,' answered King Paulus, the first of the name; 'we have not forgotten that the moist and humid air of our valley of Liddel inclines to stronger potations. Seneschal, let our faithful yeoman have a cup of brandy; it will be more germain to the matter.'

'And now,' said Mannering, 'since we have unwarily intruded upon your majesty at a moment of mirthful retirement, be pleased to say when you will indulge a stranger with an audience on those affairs of weight which have brought him to your northern capital.'

The monarch opened Mac-Morlan's letter, and, running it hastily over, exclaimed, with his natural voice and manner, 'Lucy Bertram of Ellangowan, poor dear lassie!'

'A forfeit! a forfeit!' exclaimed a dozen voices; 'his majesty has forgot his kingly character.'

'Not a whit! not a whit!' replied the king; 'I'll be judged by this courteous knight. May not a monarch love a maid of low degree? Is not King Cophetua and the Beggar-maid an adjudged case in point?'

'Professional! professional! – another forfeit,' exclaimed the tumultuary nobility.

'Had not our royal predecessors,' continued the monarch, exalting his sovereign voice to drown these disaffected clamours, – 'Had they not their Jean Logies, their Bessie Carmichaels, their Oliphants, their Sandilands, and their Weirs, and shall it be denied to us even to name a maiden whom we delight to honour? Nay, then, sink state and perish sovereignty! for, like a second Charles V., we will abdicate, and seek in the private shades of life those pleasures which are denied to a throne.'

So saying, he flung away his crown, and sprung from his exalted station with more agility than could have been expected from his age, ordered lights and a wash-hand basin and towel, with a cup of green tea, into another room, and made a sign to Mannering to accompany him. In less than two minutes he washed his face and hands, settled his wig in the glass, and, to Mannering's great surprise, looked quite a different man from the childish Bacchanal he had seen a moment before.

'There are folks,' he said, 'Mr Mannering, before whom one should take care how they play the fool – because they have either too much malice, or too little wit, as the poet says. The best compliment I can pay Colonel Mannering, is to show I am not ashamed to expose myself before him – and truly I think it is a compliment I have not spared tonight on your good-nature.'

Guy Mannering

Christopher North

A Fatal Termination

In this second extract from Christopher North's *Noctes*, the conversation turns to the life-preserving properties of drink. 'The habit of taking a glass' is once more warmly recommended by his companion, his sentimental observations again put into the mouth of the poet James Hogg, known to the author as the Ettrick Shepherd.

North. How do you like that punch, James?

Shepherd. It's rather ower sair iced, I jalouse, and will be apt to gie ane the toothache; but it has a gran' taste, and a maist seducin smell – Oh! man, that's a bonny ladle! and you hae a nice way o' steerin! Only half-fu', if you please, sir, for thae wine-glasses are perfec tummlers, and though the drink seems to be, when you are preein't, as innocent as the dew o'lauchin lassie's lip, yet it's just as dangerous, and leads insensibly on, by littles and wees, to a state o' unconscious intoxication.

Tickler. I never saw you the worse o' liquor in my life, James.

Shepherd. Nor me you.

North. None but your sober men ever get drunk.

Shepherd. I've observed that many a thousan' times; just as nane but your excessively healthy men ever die. Whene'er I hear in the kintra o' ony man's being killed aff his horse, I ken at ance that he's a sober coof, that's been gettin himsel drunk at Selkirk or Hawick, and sweein aff at a sharp turn ower the bank, he has played wallop into the water, or is aiblins been fun' lyin in the middle o' the road, wi' his neck dislocate, the doctors canna tel hoo; or ayont the wa' wi' his harns stickin on the coupin-stane.

North. Or foot in stirrup, and face trailing the pebbly mire, swept homewards by a spanking half-bred, and disentangled at the door by shriek and candle-light.

Shepherd. Had he been in the habit o' takin his glass like a Christian, he wad hae ridden like a Centaur; and instead o' havin been brought hame a corp, he wuld hae been staggerin geyan steady into the parlour, wi' a' the weans ruggin at his pouches for fairins, and his wife half angry, half pleased, helping him tidily and tenderly aff wi' his big boots; and then by-and-by mixing him the bowster cup – and then –

Tickler. Your sober man, on every public occasion of festivity, is uniformly seen, soon after 'the Duke of York and the Army,' led off between two waiters, with his face as white as the table-cloth, eyes upwards, and a ghastly smile about his gaping mouth, that seems to threaten unutterable things before he reach the lobby.

North. He turns round his head at the 'three times three,' with a loyal hiccup, and is borne off a speechless martyr to the cause of the Hanoverian Succession.

Shepherd. I wad rather get fou five hunder times in an ordinar way like, than ance to expose mysel sae afore my fellow-citizens. Yet, meet my gentleman next forenoon in the Parliament House, or in a bookseller's shop, or in Princes Street, arm-in-arm wi' a minister, and he hauds up his face as if naething had happened, speaks o' the pleasant party, expresses his regret at having been obliged to leave it so soon, at the call of a client, and, ten to ane, denounces you to his cronies for a drunkard, who exposes himself in company, and is getting constantly into scrapes that promise a fatal termination.

Noctes Ambrosianae

Allan Ramsay

Todlen Hame

Allan Ramsay (1686−1758) lived most of his life in Edinburgh where he was a leading literary figure of his day. This song in the folk tradition is from his collection of genuine, imitated and modernised folk songs, published in 1724.

Allan Ramsay

J. Smibert P.   G. Virtue S.

When I've a saxpence under my thumb,
Then I'll get credit in ilka town,
But ay when I'm poor they bid me gang by;
O! poverty parts good company.
    Todlen hame, todlen hame,
    Couldna my love come todlen hame?

Fair fa' the goodwife, and send her gude sale,
She gies us white bannocks to drink her ale,
Syne if that her tippeny chance to be sma',
We'll tak' a good scour o't and ca't awa':
    Todlen hame, todlen hame,
    As round as a neep come todlen hame.

My kimmer and I lay down to sleep,
And twa pint stoups at our bed's feet;
And ay when we waken'd, we drank them dry:
What think ye of my wee kimmer and I?
    Todlen but, and todlen ben,
    Sae round as my love comes todlen hame.

Leez me on liquor, my todlen dow,
Ye're aye sae good-humoured, when weeting your mou';
When sober, sae sour, ye'll fight with a flee,
That 'tis a blyth sight to the bairns and me,
    When todlen hame, todlen hame,
    When round as a neep you come todlen hame.

The Tea-Table Miscellany

Lord Cockburn

Social Torments

Henry Cockburn, Lord Cockburn (1779–1854), was born, and lived, in Edinburgh where he became a judge; his posthumously published *Memorials* (1856), from which this passage comes, is a mine of information about late eighteenth- and early nineteenth-century social life in that city. Among his other writings were two volumes of a *Journal*, also posthumously published (1874).

Healths and toasts were special torments; oppressions which cannot now be conceived. Every glass during dinner required to be dedicated to the health of some one. It was thought sottish and rude to take wine without this – as if forsooth there was nobody present worth drinking with. I was present, about 1803, when the late Duke of Buccleuch took a glass of sherry by himself at the table of Charles Hope, then Lord Advocate; and this was noticed afterwards as a piece of Ducal contempt. And the person asked to take wine was not invited by any thing so slovenly as a look, combined with a putting of the hand upon the bottle, as is practised by near neighbours now. It was a much more serious affair. For one thing, the wine was very rarely on the table. It had to be called for; and in order to let the servant know to whom he was to carry it, the caller was obliged to specify his partner aloud. All this required some premeditation and courage. Hence timid men never ventured on so bold a step at all; but were glad to escape by only drinking when they were invited. As this ceremony was a mark of respect, the landlord, or any other person who thought himself the great man, was generally graciously pleased to perform it to every one present. But he and others were always at liberty to abridge the severity of the duty, by performing it by platoons. They took a brace, or two brace, of ladies or of gentlemen, or of both, and got them all engaged at once, and proclaiming to the sideboard – 'A glass of sherry for Miss Dundas, Mrs Murray, and Miss Hope, and a glass of port for Mr Hume, and one for me,' he slew them by coveys. And all the parties to the contract were bound to acknowledge each other distinctly. No nods, or grins, or indifference; but a direct look at the object, the audible uttering of the very words – 'Your good health,' accompanied by a respectful inclination of the head, a gentle attraction of the right hand towards the heart, and a gratified smile. And

53

after all these detached pieces of attention during the feast were over, no sooner was the table cleared, and the after dinner glasses set down, than it became necessary for each person, following the landlord, to drink the health of every other person present, individually. Thus, where there were ten people, there were ninety healths drunk. This ceremony was often slurred over by the bashful, who were allowed merely to *look* the benediction; but usage compelled them to look it distinctly, and to each individual. To do this well, required some grace, and consequently it was best done by the polite ruffled and frilled gentlemen of the olden time.

This prandial nuisance was horrible. But it was nothing to what followed. For after dinner, and before the ladies retired, there generally began what were called '*Rounds*' of toasts; when each gentleman named an absent lady, and each lady an absent gentleman, separately; or one person was required to give an absent lady, and another person was required to match a gentleman with that lady, and the pair named were toasted, generally with allusions and jokes about the fitness of the union. And, worst of all, there were 'Sentiments.' These were short epigrammatic sentences, expressive of moral feelings and virtues, and were thought refined and elegant productions. A faint conception of their nauseousness may be formed from the following examples, every one of which I have heard given a thousand times, and which indeed I only recollect from their being favourites. The glasses being filled, a person was asked for his, or for her, sentiment, when this or something similar was committed – 'May the pleasures of the evening bear the reflections of the morning.' Or, 'May the friends of our youth be the companions of our old age.' Or, 'Delicate pleasures to susceptible minds.' 'May the honest heart never feel distress.' 'May the hand of charity wipe the tear from the eye of sorrow.' 'May never worse be among us.' There were stores of similar reflections; and for all kinds of parties, from the elegant and romantic, to the political, the municipal, the ecclesiastic, and the drunken. Many of the thoughts and sayings survive still, and may occasionally be heard at a club or a tavern. But even there they are out of vogue as established parts of the entertainment; and in some scenes nothing can be very offensive. But the proper *sentiment* was a high and pure production; a moral motto; and was meant to dignify and grace private society. Hence, even after an easier age began to sneer at the display, the correct course was to receive the sentiment, if not with real admiration, at least with decorous respect. Mercifully, there was a large known public stock of the odious commodity, so that nobody who could screw up his nerves to pronounce the words, had any occasion to strain his invention. The conceited, the ready, or the reckless, hackneyed in the art, had a knack of making new sentiments applicable to the passing accidents, with great ease. But it was a dreadful oppression on the timid or the awkward. They used to shudder, ladies particularly – for nobody was spared, when their turn in the *round* approached. Many a struggle and blush did it cost; but this seemed only to excite the tyranny of the masters of the craft; and compliance could never be avoided except by more torture than yielding.

Memorials of His Time

Edward Gaitens

Jimmy Macdonnel Comes Home from Sea

Edward Gaitens (1897–1966) was born in the Gorbals, Glasgow, and contributed sketches of Glasgow slum life to the *Scots Magazine*. Some of them were incorporated into this novel, published in 1948. Gaitens left school at the age of fourteen and was a genuine working-class writer.

Every time Jimmy Macdonnel came home from sea there was a party and a few more after it till his pay of several months was burned right up. Even if Mrs Macdonnel had been six months teetotal she couldn't resist taking one wee nip to celebrate her son's return and that wee nip somehow multiplied, had bairns, as she would laughingly tell you herself.

Returning from his last voyage before the Great War, Jimmy Macdonnel, after a year's absence as cook on a tramp steamship, was the originator of a famous Macdonnel party. It was a bright July Saturday afternoon when Jimmy unexpectedly arrived. A delicious smell of Irish stew was still hanging around the Macdonnel kitchen. Mrs Macdonnel was a rare cook and Mr Macdonnel who loved her cooking had dropped into a smiling drowse, dazed by his enormous meal.

Just then there was a knock at the stairhead door and Mrs Macdonnel, touching back her greying, reddish hair rose in a fluster to open, exclaimed. 'My Goad, it's Jimmy!' and returned followed by a slim, dapper young man of twenty-nine, with bronzed features, in the uniform of a petty-officer of the Merchant Service and carrying a sailor's kitbag which he dumped on the floor.

'Did ye no' ken Ah was comin' hame the day?', he asked resentfully; 'Ah, sent ye a postcard fae Marsels.'

'Och, no son!' said his mother, blaming in her heart those 'forrin' post-cairds' which always bewildered her. 'Shure yer da would hiv come tae meet the boat. Ye said the twenty-seeventh,' and she began searching in a midget bureau on the dresser to prove her words, then she gazed mystified at the 'Carte Postale' with the view of Marseilles Harbour. 'Och, Ah'm haverin'!' she cried, 'it says here the seeventeenth!'

'Ach away! Ye're daft!' said Jimmy, 'How could ye mistake a "one" for a "two"!'

Mr Macdonnel woke up, rubbing his eyes, Eddy got down from the dishboard, closing his Grammar; and they all stared at Jimmy in silent wonder. He certainly looked trim as a yacht in his blue reefer suit, white shirt, collar and black tie, but they weren't amazed at his spruceness nor by his unexpected arrival but by the fact that he stood there as sober as a priest. For ten years Jimmy had been coming home from sea at varying intervals and had never been able to get up the stairs unassisted; and here he was, after a six months voyage, not even giving off a smell of spirits. Mr Macdonnel put on his glasses to have a better look at him. What was wrong with Jimmy? They wondered if he was ill, then the agonising thought that he had been robbed occurred simultaneously to the old folk, and Jimmy was about to ask them what they were all look-ing at when his mother collected herself and embraced him and his father shook his hand, patting his shoulder.

Jimmy flushed with annoyance at his mother's sentiment as he pro-duced from his kitbag a large plug of ship's tobacco for his da, a Spanish shawl of green silk, with big crimson roses on it for his mother, and a coloured plaster-of-paris plaque of Cologne Cathedral for his Aunt Kate, then, blushing slightly, he took his seaman's book from his pocket and showed them the photograph of a young woman, 'That's Meg,' he said, 'Meg Macgregor. She's a fisher-girl. I met her at the herring-boats when me ship called in at Peterhead.'

His mother was delighted with his taste and knew immediately why he had arrived sober. She passed the photograph to her husband, who beamed at it and said heartily, 'My, she's a stunner, Jimmy boy! A pro-per stunner! She'll create a sensation roun' here!' Mr Macdonnel usually awoke ill-tempered from his after-dinner naps, but his indigestion van-ished like magic as he imagined the glorious spree they were going to have on Jimmy's six months' pay; and he swore he had never seen such a beautiful young woman as Meg Macgregor. Then Jimmy startled them all by announcing, as if he was forcing it out of himself: 'Meg's awfu' good-livin', mother, an' she's asked me tae stoap drinkin' for the rest o' ma life. Ah've promised her Ah will.'

Mr Macdonnel glared wildly at his son, then gave a sour look at the portrait and, handing it back without a word, rolled down his sleeves and pulled up his braces. He was dumbfounded. What had come over his son Jimmy? Teetotal for the rest of his life! Was he going to lose his head over that silly-faced girl? Mrs Macdonnel studied Jimmy with plain-tive anxiety while he described Meg's beauty and goodness. 'Ach, she was made tae be adored b' everybody!' he said, and warned his mother to steer clear of the drink and keep her house in order to receive his beloved, whom he had invited to come and stay with the family.

His mother promised to love Meg as a daughter and silently hoped that the girl would stay at home. She was too old now to be bothered by a healthy young woman with managing ways. Jimmy swore he hadn't touched a drop since he had sailed from Peterhead and described the tortures of his two-days' self-denial so vividly that his father shivered and hurried into the parlour to get his coat and vest. Jimmy said he was finished with the sea and booze; sick of squandering money. He was determined to settle on shore, get married, and spend all his money on Meg's happiness.

A miserly gleam beamed in his mother's eye when he said that and she wondered how much his new devotion would limit his contribution to her purse. Jimmy took a bundle of notes from his inside breast pocket and handed her thirty pounds, reminding her that she had already drawn advance sums from his shipping-office. Mrs Macdonnel said he was too kind and offered to return five notes with a drawing-back movement, but Jimmy refused them with a bluff insincere gesture, for there was a flash of regret in his eye as she tucked the wad in her purse, but, with genuine feeling he invited her and his da out to drink him welcome home. 'Ah'll have a lemonade,' he said, gazing piously at the ceiling as though at the Holy Grail. His mother thought he was being too harsh with himself. 'Shure ye'll hiv a wee nip wi' me an' yer da, son. A wee nip won't kill ye!' she laughed slyly, and Jimmy promised to drink a shandygaff just to please her, sighing with relief when he thought of the dash of beer in the lemonade. He called his father who came in from the parlour wrestling with a white dickey which he was trying to dispose evenly on his chest. 'Ah won't keep ye a jiffy, laddie!' he said, facing the mirror and fervently praying that the smell of the pub would restore poor Jimmy to his senses.

As she put on her old brown shawl Mrs Macdonnel was disappointed at Jimmy's insistence that they should go to an out-of-the-way pub. She wanted to show off her bonny son; he was so braw; so like a captain! She imagined the greetings they would get going down the long street.

'Ay, ye've won hame, Jimmy, boay? My, ye're lookin' fine, mun! Goash, ye oaght tae be a prood wumman the day, Mrs Macdonnel! Jimmy's a credit tae ye!' and she foretasted the old sweet thrill of envy and flattery. But Jimmy said he would never drink again with the corner-boys. Love had made a new man of him!

When they had all gone out Eddy Macdonnel hurried into the small side bedroom to read the book on PSYCHOLOGY AND MORALS he had borrowed from the Corporation Library. Inspired by Jimmy's miraculous conversion he crouched over the volume, concentrating fiercely on the chapters headed WILL POWER AND SIN, and his heart swelled with a reformer's zeal as he saw himself one day applying all these marvellous laws to the human race, hypnotising countless millions of people into sobriety.

Three hours later he heard a loud clamour in the street below. Throwing his book on the bed he raised the window and looked over and his uplifted heart sank down, for he saw Jimmy stumbling happily up the street with his Aunt Kate's hat on his head and his arm round his father's neck. They were lustily singing 'The Bonny Lass O' Ballochmyle.' Mr Macdonnel's dickey was sticking out like the wings of a moulted swan and large bottles of whisky waggled from the pockets of the two men. Behind them, laughing like witches, came Mrs Macdonnel and Aunt Kate with the sailor's cap on, followed by six of Jimmy's pals who were carrying between them three large crates of bottled beer.

Eddy closed the window quickly and stared sadly at the wall. Jimmy, the idol of his dream, himself had shattered it! As he turned into the lobby, Jimmy opened the stairhead door and thrust his pals into the kitchen, which already seemed crowded with only two members of the family. John Macdonnel, now a fair young man of twenty-five, just home from overtime at the shipyards, leant in his oilstained working clothes against the gas stove, reading about the Celtic and Rangers match in the Glasgow Evening Times and regretting that he had missed a hard-fought game which his team had won. With a wild 'whoopee' Jimmy embraced his brothers, who smiled with embarrassment. John was proud of Jimmy's prestige with the corner boys, though he knew it was the worthless esteem for a fool and his money; Eddy saw Jimmy as a grand romantic figure, a great chef who had cooked for a millionaire on his yacht and had seen all the capital cities of the world, and Jimmy's kitbag, lying against a home-made stool by the dresser, stuffed with cook's caps and jackets, radiated the fascination of travel.

Aunt Kate, a tiny, dark woman of remarkable vitality, went kissing all her nephews in turn and the party got into full swing. Liquor was soon winking from tumblers, tea-cups, egg-cups – anything that could hold drink – and Aunt Kate, while directing the young men to bring chairs from the parlour, sang 'A Guid New Year Tae Ane An' A',' disregarding the fact that it was only summer time, and Jimmy, thinking a nautical song was expected from him, sang 'A Life On The Ocean Wave!' in a voice as flat as stale beer that drowned his Aunt's pleasant treble. But somebody shouted that he sang as well as John McCormack and he sat down with a large tumbler of whisky, looking as if he thought so himself.

Then Aunt Kate told everybody about her marvellous meeting with Jimmy whose voice she had heard through the partition as she sat in the Ladies' Parlour in The Rob Roy Arms and Eddy learned how his brother had fallen. Jimmy, it appeared, felt he must toast Meg Macgregor in just one glass of something strong; that dash of beer in lemonade had infuriated his thirst and in a few minutes he had downed several glasses of the right stuff to his sweetheart, proving to his aunt's delight that he was still the same old jovial Jimmy.

John Macdonnel, all this while, was going to and fro, stumbling over outthrust feet between the small bedroom and kitchen sprucing himself up to go out and meet his girl. From feet to waist he was ready for love. His best brown trousers with shoes to match adorned his lower half, while his torso was still robed in a shirt blackened with shipyard oil and rust. He washed himself at the sink, laughing at his Aunt's story, then turned, drying himself, to argue with his mother about his 'clean change.' Mrs Macdonnel waved her cup helplessly, saying she couldn't help the indifference of laundrymen and John implored Eddy to shoot downstairs and find if the family washing had arrived at the receiving-office of the Bonnyburn Laundries.

Visitors kept dropping in for a word with the sailor and delayed their departure while the drinks went round. Rumour had spread the report that Jimmy Macdonnel was home flush with money and a Macdonnel party was always a powerful attraction. The gathering was livening up. Two quart bottles of whisky had been absorbed and beer was frothing against every lip when Eddy returned triumphantly waving a big brown paper parcel in John's direction.

It was at the right psychological moment, when a slight lull in the merriment was threatening, that Rab Macpherson romped from his hiding-place in the doorway into the middle of the kitchen and suddenly burst out singing at the top of his voice:

'Le – et Kings an' courteers rise an' fa'
This wurrld has minny turns,
But brighter beams abune them a'
The star o' Rabbie Burns!'

Rab's legs were very bow and wee Tommy Mohan, who was talking to his pal John Macdonnel at the sink, sunk down on his hunkers and gazed under his palm, like a sailor looking over the sea, away through Rab's legs all the time he was singing. Everybody was convulsed with laughter and Mrs Macdonnel was so pleased with Rab, that she got up, still laughing, and with her arm around his neck, gave him a good measure of whisky in a small cream jug.

Suddenly everybody fell silent to listen to Jimmy Macdonnel, who had been up since three that morning and half-asleep was trolling away to himself, 'The Lass That Made The Bed For Me' and Mrs Steedman, a big-bosomed Orangewoman, startled the company by shouting, 'Good aul' Rabbie Burns! He ken't whit a wumman likes the maist!' There was a roar of laughter at this reminder of the poet's lechery, then Aunt Kate insisted that Mr Macdonnel should sing, 'I Dreamt That I Dwelt In Marble Halls,' while her sister, Mrs Macdonnel, asked him for 'The Meeting Of The Waters' because it reminded her of their honeymoon in Ireland. Mr Macdonnel, assisted by the table, swayed to his feet as pompously as Signor Caruso, twirled his moustache, stuck his thumbs behind his lapels, like the buskers of Glasgow backcourts, and 'hem-med' very loudly to silence the arguing sisters. He always sang with his eyes closed and when the gaslight shone on his glasses he looked like a man with four eyes, one pair shut, the other brilliantly open. He honestly believed he had a fine tenor voice and with swelled chest he bellowed:

'Yes! Let me like a soldier fall, upon some open plain!
Me breast boldly bared to meet the ball
That blots out every stain!'

The china shivered on the shelves above the dresser and Eddy Mac-donnel, lost in some vision of bravery, stared with pride at his father. Halfway through the ballad, Mr Macdonnel forgot the words but sang on, 'tra-laing' here, pushing in his own words there, and sat down well satisfied to a din of handclaps and stamping feet.

Jimmy was blasted into wakefulness by his father's song and he washed himself sober and led out all the young men to help him buy more drink. When they returned, well-stocked, half-an-hour later, Mr Macdonnel had the whole crowd singing.

'I'll knock a hole in McCann for knocking a hole in me can!
McCann knew me can was new
I'd only had it a day or two,
I gave McCann me can to fetch me a pint of stout
An' McCann came running in an said
That me can was running out!'

This was Mr Macdonnel's winning number at every spree and the re-frain had echoed several times through the open windows to the street and backcourt before the young men returned. In the comparative silence of clinking bottles and glasses, Jimmy told his laughing guests of the night when he had served up beer in chamber-pots to a party of corner-boys. A dozen chamber-pots were arrayed round the table and twelve youths sat gravely before them while Jimmy muttered a Turkish grace over the beer and told them that was the way the Turks drank their drink and they believed him because he had been six times round the world.

When Aunt Kate had recovered from her delight in this story she asked Eddy to run up and see if her 'bonny wee man' was home from the gasworks. Eddy raced up to the top storey, knocked on a door, and started back as his uncle's gargoyle face thrust out at him and barked, 'Where's Katey? Am Oi a man or a mouse? B' the Holy Saint Pathrick Oi'll murther the lazy cow!' Eddy said faintly, 'Jimmy's home an' we're having a party. Will ye come down?' and Mr Hewes followed him down-stairs muttering threats of vengeance on his wife for neglecting his tea.

The gathering had overflowed into the parlour when Eddy returned with the gasworker behind him; the lobby was crowded with newly-arrived guests listening to Aunt Kate singing 'The Irish Emigrant's Fare-well;' the eyes of all the women were wet with film-star tears and the singer herself seemed to be seeing a handsome Irish youth as she looked straight at her husband standing in the kitchen doorway and returning her stare with a malignant leer. Aunt Kate filled a large cup with whisky from a bottle on the dresser and, still singing, handed it to him with a mock bow. On similar occasions Mr Hewes had been known to dash the cup from her hand and walk out and desert her for six months, but this time he seized it, swallowed the drink in one gulp, hitched up his belt and joined the party.

Eddy crushed a way through to his seat on the sink and watched his uncle, who, seated beside Mr Macdonnel, eyed with hostility every move of his popular wife. There was an excess of spite in Mr Hewes and he loved to hate people. Time, accident and ill-nature had ruined his face. A livid scar streamed from his thin hair down his right temple to his lip; his broken nose had reset all to one side, his few teeth were black and his little moustache as harsh as barbed wire; and with a blackened sweatrag round his neck he looked like a being from some underworld come to spy on human revels. He was called upon for a song when the applause for his wife had ended, and he stood up and roared, glaring at her:

'Am Oi a man, or am Oi a mouse
Or am I a common artful dodger?
Oi want to know who is master of my house!
Is ut me or Micky Flanagan the lodger?'

Shouts of 'ongcore!' egged him on to sing the verse several times, his glare at his smiling wife intensifying with each repetition. He was suspected of having composed the song himself and the neighbours always knew he was going to desert his wife when he came up the stairs singing it. His whole body was humming like a dynamo after two large cups of Heather Dew and as his wife began chanting an old Irish jig he started to dance. Throwing off his jacket he roared 'B' Jasus!' tightened his belt and rolled up his sleeves, revealing thick leather straps round his wrists, and his hob-nailed boots beat a rapid deafening tattoo on the spot of floor inside the surrounding feet. His wife's chant became shriller and the whole company began clapping hands, stamping and yelling wild 'hoochs!' that drove the little gasworker to frenzy. John Macdonnel, all dressed to go out with a new bowler hat perched on his head, lifted a poker from the grate and thrust it into the dancer's hand. Mr Hewes tried to twirl it round his head between finger and thumb like a drum-major, then smashed it on the floor in passionate chagrin at his failure. 'B' Jasus Oi could dance ye'se all under the table!' he yelled, and with head and torso held stiff and arms working like pistons across his middle, he pranced like an enraged cockerel.

Faster he hopped from heel to heel, still packed with energy after a hard day shovelling in a hot atmosphere; sweat glistened on his grey hair and beaded his blackened cheeks; he twisted his feet in and out in awkward attempts at fancy steps and looked as if he would fly asunder in his efforts to beat the pace of his accompanists; then, with a despairing yell of 'B' Jasus!' he stopped suddenly, gasped, 'Och, Oi'm bate!' and hurled dizzily behind foremost into his chair.

It was a hefty piece of furniture but it couldn't stand up to his violence; with a loud crack its four legs splayed out and the gasworker crashed like a slung sack into the hearth, smashing the polished plate-shelf sticking out beneath the oven; his head struck heavily the shining bevel of the range; the snapped chair-back lay over his head, and there was a roar of laughter which stopped when he was seen to lie still among the wreckage.

His wife and Mr Macdonnel bent over him, but he pushed them away, staggered erect and, shaking himself like a dog after a fight, snatched and swallowed the cup of whisky which Mrs Macdonnel had poured quickly for him while looking ruefully at her shattered chair and plate-shelf. The blow had hardly affected him and, as Mrs Hewes anxiously examined his head he pushed her rudely aside, shouting, 'B' Jasus! Oi'll give ye'se 'The Enniskillen's Farewell!' and he roared boastfully the Boer War song of an Irish regiment's departure. Suddenly he realized that attention was diverted from him; someone in the packed lobby was crying, 'Here's Big Mary! Make way for Blind Mary!' and Mr Hewes, grasping his jacket from Mr Macdonnel's hand, slung it across his shoulder, stared malignantly at everyone and pushed uncivilly out of the house.

The Widow Loughran, who was being guided in by Jerry Delaney and his wife, was a magnificent Irishwoman, well over six feet, round about forty, and round about considerably more at waist and bosom. The habit of raising the head in the manner of the blind made her appear taller and gave her a haughty look, but she was a jolly, kind woman in robust health, and her rosy face and glossy, jet hair, her good-humoured laughter, caused one to forget her blindness. Blind Mary was the wonder of the Gorbals. She drank hard and regularly and stood it better than the toughest men. 'Mary's never up nor doon,' they said, and she boasted that she had never known a 'bad moarnin'' in her life. She also wore a tartan shoulder-shawl of the Gordon clan, a widow's bonnet, and a bright print apron over her skirt. Mrs Macdonnel led her to a seat and she stood up, her hands searching around for Jerry Delaney when she heard there wasn't a chair for him. He was pushed into her arms and she pulled him into a tight embrace on her ample knees. Mr Delaney, popularly known as 'One-Eyed Jerry' since a flying splinter, at his work as a ship's carpenter, had deprived him of his right eye, was no light weight, but Mary handled him like a baby, and Mrs Macdonnel shrieked with laughter: 'Blind Mary's stole yer man, Bridget!' and Mrs Delaney, a dark beauty of five-and-thirty, laughed back, 'Ach away! She's welcome tae him! Shure they're weel matched wi' yin eye atween them!' This so tickled Mary and Jerry that they almost rolled on the floor with helpless laughter, and Mrs Macdonnel looked very worried, expecting every minute to see another of her chairs smashed to smithereens.

Aunt Kate had vanished in pursuit of her man and returned at this moment, pale with anger, to announce publicly that he had skedaddled, but that she would set the police at his heels and make him support her; then she sang in her sweetest voice, 'O My Love Is Like A Red, Red

Rose!' followed by a delicate rendering of 'Ae Fond Kiss.' But no one was surprised by her instant change from wrath to tenderness, except young Eddy, who felt that this was his most profitable 'psychological' evening as he watched Blind Mary with her hands boldly grasping Mr Delaney's thighs and began excitedly composing an essay on 'Psychology And The Blind' for his night-school class.

Someone called for a song from Blind Mary, and One-Eyed Jerry courteously handed her to her feet. She stood dominating the whole room, protesting that she couldn't sing a note, but everyone cried: 'Strike up, Mary! Ye sing like a lark!' And she began singing 'Bonny Mary O' Argyle' to the unfailing amazement of young Eddy, who could never understand why her voice that was so melodious in speech was so hideous when she sang. In his boyhood Eddy had always loved to see her in the house, finding a strange sense of comfort in her strength and cheerful vitality. Coming in from school his heart had always rippled with delight to see her gossiping and drinking with his mother and some neighbours. Her rich brogue always welcomed him, 'Ach, it's me wee Edward. Come here, ye darlin'!' and there was always a penny or six-penny bit for him, hot from her fat hand, or a bag of sweets, warm from her placket-pocket, their colours blushing through the paper. He enjoyed the strong smell of snuff from her soft fingers when they fondled his hair or read his face and the smell of her kiss, scented with whisky or beer, had never repelled him.

Mary had only sung two lines when she was sensationally interrupted by Bridget Delaney, who suddenly leapt from her feet and shrieked indignantly: 'Ach, don't talk tae me aboot legs! Is there a wumman in this house has a better leg than meself? Tae hell wi' Bonny Mary O' Argyle! I'll show ye'se the finest leg on the South Side this night!' and she bent and pulled her stocking down her left leg to the ankle, whipped up her blue satinette skirt and pulled up a blue leg of bloomer so fiercely that she revealed a handsome piece of behind. 'There ye are!' cried Bridget, holding forth her leg. 'Ah defy a wumman among ye'se tae shake as good a wan!'

Blind Mary stood silent and trembling in a strange listening attitude, thinking a fight had begun, and everyone was astounded. Jerry Delaney, blushing with shame, plucked nervously at his bedfellow's skirt, but Bridget pulled it up more tightly and shouted: 'Awa! Ye've seen it oaften enough! Are ye ashamed o' it?' while Jerry told her he had always said she had the finest leg in Glasgow and acted as if he had never beheld such a distressing sight. Beside them a very dozy youth gazed dully at Bridget's fat, white thigh, and from the rose-wreathed wallpaper Pope Pius X, in a cheap print, looked sternly at the sinful limb.

Mrs Macdonnel hurried her hysterical sister-in-law into the small bedroom, and the only comment on the incident was, 'Blimey! Wot a

65

lark!' from Mrs Bills. Blind Mary asked excitedly what had happened. Some of the ladies, while affecting shocked modesty, trembled with desire to take up Bridget's challenge; but no one could have explained her hysteria, except, perhaps, Mr Delaney. His one eye always glowed with admiration for a fine woman and he had gazed warmly all evening at Blind Mary. But Bridget's astonishing behaviour was superseded for the moment by the arrival of Wee Danny Quinn 'wi' his melodyin',' whom Jimmy Macdonnel himself introduced as the guest of honour.

The street-musician, a pugnosed, dwarfish Glaswegian, bowlegged and very muscular, drank two large glasses of whisky, wiped his lips and began playing. The mother-o'-pearl keys of his big Lombardi piano-accordeon flashed in the gaslight as his fingers danced skilfully among them, and while he leant his ear to the instrument, his little dark eyes looked up with a set smile, like a leprechaun listening to the earth. He played jigs and reels and waltzes; all the furniture in the kitchen was pushed to the wall and all who could find room to crush around were soon dancing through the lobby and back again.

It was late in the night, when the dancers had paused for refreshment, that Willie McBride the bookmaker, a six-foot red-headed Highlandman, suddenly reappeared arm-in-arm with his wife, he dressed in her clothes and she in his. They had disappeared for fifteen minutes and affected the change with the connivance of Aunt Kate, who slipped them the key of her house. Mr McBride had somehow managed to crush his enormous chest into the blouse of his slim wife; between it and the skirt, his shirt looked out, and from the edge of the skirt, which reached his knees, his thick, pink woollen drawers were visible; Mrs McBride, drowned in his suit, floundered, bowing to the delighted company.

This wild whim of the McBrides heated everyone like an aphrodisiac, and very soon Aunt Kate's but-an'-ben became the dressing-room for the transformation of several ladies and gentlemen. The two Delaneys exchanged clothes and Bridget showed to advantage her splendid legs swelling out her husband's trousers; Aunt Kate retired with a slight youth and reappeared in his fifty-shilling suit as the neatest little man of the evening; then Mrs Macdonnel walked in disguised as her husband, even to his glasses and cap, and was followed by him gallantly wearing the Spanish shawl, in which, after filling out his wife's blouse with two towels, he danced what he imagined was a Spanish dance and sang a hashed-up version of the 'Toreador Song' from Carmen.

Danny Quinn's playing became inspired and his volume majestic as he laughed at the dressed-up couples dancing around. The house was throbbing like a battered drum when heavy thumps shook the stair-head door. 'It's the polis,' cried everyone with amused alarm. Mrs Macdonnel rushed to open and a soft Irish voice echoed along the lobby: 'Ye'se'll have to make less noise. The nayburs is complainin'!'

'Ach, come awa in, Tarry, an' have a wee deoch-an'-doris!' cried Mrs Macdonnel, holding the door wide for the portly constable who stood amazed at her masculine garb, while Willie McBride was roaring, 'Do Ah hear me aul' freend Boab Finnegan? Come ben an' have a drink, man! Shure you an' me's had many a dram when yer inspector wisnae lookin'!' and Mrs Macdonnel conducted into the parlour police-officer Finnegan followed by a tall, young Highland officer, a novice in the Force, with finger at chinstrap and a frown of disapproval. The two policemen were welcomed with full glasses, and Mr Finnegan, known all over The Gorbals as 'Tarry Bob' because his hair and big moustache were black as tar and his heavy jowls became more saturnine with every shave he had, surveyed the strange gathering with a clownish smile, while Mr McBride, the street bookie, told the company how often he had dodged the Law by giving Tarry Bob a friendly drink.

In five minutes both policemen sat down and laid their helmets on the sideboard among the numerous bottles and fifteen minutes later they had loosened their tunics and were dancing with the ladies, their heavy boots creating a louder rumpus than they had come to stop.

Eddy Macdonnel stood in the crowded lobby craning his head over to watch the lively scene. After a long while he heard his mother say to Tarry Bob, who was protesting he must go: 'Och, hiv another wee nip! Shure a wee nip won't kill ye!' then he saw the good-natured policeman drench himself in beer as he put on his helmet into which some playful guest had emptied a pint bottle.

Eddy's wits were staggering. 'Human behaviour' had passed his understanding. In a state of bewilderment he opened the stairhead door and wandered slowly down to the closemouth. His confused head was ringing with a medley of folk-songs and music-hall choruses and his heart held the streams and hills and the women of the poetry of Robert Burns. He was thinking of Jeannie Lindsay and wishing he might find her standing at her close in South Wellington Street. But it was very late. He hurried round the corner in a queer, emotional tangle of sexual shame and desire, his romantic thoughts of Jeannie mingled with the shameful memory of his mother and the women dressing up in men's clothes and Bridget Delaney pulling up her skirts to her hips to show her bare legs to the men.

Dance of the Apprentices

George Outram

Drinkin' Drams

George Outram (1805–56) was editor of *The Glasgow Herald* between 1837 and 1856. His collection of poems, *Lyrics, Legal and Miscellaneous*, appeared in 1874.

He ance was holy
An' melancholy,
Till he found the folly
    O singin' psalms;
He's now red's a rose,
And there's pimples on his nose,
And in size it daily grows
    By drinkin' drams.

He ance was weak,
An' couldnae eat a steak
Wi' out gettin' sick
    An' takin' qualms;
But now he can eat
O ony kind o meat,
For he's got an appeteet
    By drinkin' drams.

He ance was thin,
Wi' a nose like a pen,
An haunds like a hen,
    An' nae hams;
But now he's round and tight,
And a deevil o a wight,
For he's got himsel' put right
    By drinkin' drams.

He ance was soft as dirt,
And as pale as ony shirt,
And as useless as a cart
    Wi' out the trams;
But now he'd race the deil,
Or swallow Jonah's whale –
He's as gleg's a puddock's tail
    Wi' drinkin' drams.

Oh! pale, pale was his hue,
And cauld, cauld was his broo,
An' he grumbled like a ewe
    Mang libbit rams;
But noo his broo is bricht,
An' his een are orbs o licht,
An' his nose is just a sicht
    Wi' drinkin' drams.

He studied mathematics,
Logic, ethics, hydrostatics,
Till he needed diuretics
    To lowse his dams;
But now, wi'out a lee,
He could mak' anither sea,
For he's left philosophy
    An' taen to drams.

He found that learnin', fame,
Gas, philanthropy and steam,
Logic, loyalty, gude name,
    Were a' mere shams;
That the source o joy below,
An' the antidote to woe,
And the only proper go,
    Was drinkin' drams.

Lyrics, Legal and Miscellaneous

Lord Cockburn

Under The Table

The subject of this engaging piece of nostalgia from Lord Cockburn's *Journal* is Henry Mackenzie (1745–1831), whose novel *The Man of Feeling* (1771), much admired by Burns, was widely read and highly thought of in his day.

On my way from Inverness we paid a visit at Kilravock Castle. It is a delightful place, and we were most hospitably entertained. The quantity of wine, however, the party consumed happened to be singularly small, and I could not help thinking of the very different days that the Tower had seen; for it was at Kilravock that old Henry Mackenzie, who was related to the family, used to tell that a sort of household officer was kept, whose duty was to prevent the drunk guests from choking. Mackenzie was once at a festival there, towards the close of which the exhausted topers sank gradually back and down on their chairs, till little of them was seen above the table except their noses; and at last they disappeared altogether and fell on the floor. Those who were too far gone to rise lay still there from necessity; while those who, like the *Man of Feeling*, were glad of a pretence for escaping fell into a dose from policy. While Mackenzie was in this state he was alarmed by feeling a hand working about his throat, and called out. A voice answered, 'Dinna be feared, Sir; it's me.' 'And who are you?' 'A'm the lad that louses the craavats.'

Journal of Henry Cockburn

James Boswell

A Hangover in the Hebrides

Boswell's classic account of his accompanying Dr Johnson in his tour of the Western Isles of Scotland in August—October 1773 is full of revealing details about the behaviour of both himself and his companion. Boswell is never ashamed to expose his own weaknesses.

Dr Johnson went to bed soon. When one bowl of punch was finished, I rose, and was near the door, in my way up stairs to bed; but Corri-chatachin said, it was the first time Col had been in his house, and he should have his bowl; – and would not I join in drinking it? The hearti-ness of my honest landlord, and the desire of doing social honour to

71

our very obliging conductor, induced me to sit down again. *Col's* bowl was finished; and by that time we were well warmed. A third bowl was soon made, and that too was finished. We were cordial, and merry to a high degree; but of what passed I have no recollection, with any accuracy. I remember calling *Corrichatachin* by the familiar appellation of *Corri*, which his friends do. A fourth bowl was made, by which time *Col*, and young M'Kinnon, Corrichatachin's son, slipped away to bed. I continued a little with *Corri* and *Knockow*; but at last I left them. It was near five in the morning when I got to bed.

Sunday, 26th September

I awaked at noon, with a severe head-ach. I was much vexed that I should have been guilty of such a riot, and afraid of a reproof from Dr Johnson. I thought it very inconsistent with that conduct which I ought to maintain, while the companion of the *Rambler*. About one he came into my room, and accosted me, 'What, drunk yet?' – His tone of voice was not that of severe upbraiding; so I was relieved a little. – 'Sir, said I, they kept me up.' – He answered, 'No, you kept them up, you drunken dog:' – This he said with good-humoured *English* pleasantry. Soon afterwards, Corrichatachin, Col, and other friends assembled round my bed. *Corri* had a brandy-bottle and glass with him, and insisted I should take a dram. – 'Ay, said Dr Johnson, fill him drunk again. Do it in the morning, that we may laugh at him all day. It is a poor thing for a fellow to get drunk at night, and sculk to bed, and let his friends have no sport.' – Finding him thus jocular, I became quite easy; and when I offered to get up, he very good-naturedly said, 'You need be in no such hurry now.' – I took my host's advice, and drank some brandy, which I found an effectual cure for my head-ach. When I rose, I went into Dr Johnson's room, and taking up Mrs M'Kinnon's Prayer-book, I opened it at the twentieth Sunday after Trinity, in the epistle for which I read, 'And be not drunk with wine, wherein there is excess.' Some would have taken this as a divine interposition.

Journal of a Tour to the Hebrides with Samuel Johnson LL.D.

Robert Burns

Tam in the Pub

This is the opening of Burns's great narrative poem, which puts into vigorous Scots verse of varying speed and colour the story of an encounter with witches by a drunken Ayrshireman returning home from an evening's drinking. The story is based on an old folk tale, and Burns wrote it at the request of the antiquary Francis Grose.

When chapman billies leave the street,
And drouthy neebors neebors meet;
As market-days are wearing late,
An' folk begin to tak the gate;
While we sit bousing at the nappy,
An' getting fou and unco happy,
We think na on the lang Scots miles,
The mosses, waters, slaps, and styles,
That lie between us and our hame,
Whare sits our sulky, sullen dame,
Gathering her brows like gathering storm,
Nursing her wrath to keep it warm.

This truth fand honest Tam o' Shanter,
As he frae Ayr ae night did canter:
(Auld Ayr, wham ne'er a town surpasses,
For honest men and bonie lasses.)

O Tam, had'st thou but been sae wise,
As taen thy ain wife Kate's advice!
She tauld thee weel thou was a skellum,
A blethering, blustering, drunken blellum;
That frae November till October,
Ae market-day thou was nae sober;
That ilka melder wi' the miller,
Thou sat as lang as thou had siller;
That ev'ry naig was ca'd a shoe on,
The smith and thee gat roaring fou on;
That at the Lord's house, even on Sunday,
Thou drank wi' Kirkton Jean till Monday.
She prophesied, that, late or soon,
Thou would be found deep drown'd in Doon,
Or catch'd wi' warlocks in the mirk
By Alloway's auld, haunted kirk.

Ah! gentle dames, it gars me greet,
To think how monie counsels sweet,
How monie lengthen'd, sage advices
The husband frae the wife despises!

But to our tale: Ae market-night,
Tam had got planted unco right,
Fast by an ingle, bleezing finely,
Wi' reaming swats, that drank divinely;
And at his elbow, Souter Johnie,
His ancient, trusty, drouthy cronie:
Tam lo'ed him like a very brither;
They had been fou for weeks thegither.
The night drave on wi' sangs and clatter;
And ay the ale was growing better:
The landlady and Tam grew gracious
Wi' secret favours, sweet and precious:
The Souter tauld his queerest stories;
The landlord's laugh was ready chorus:
The storm without might rair and rustle,
Tam did na mind the storm a whistle.

Care, mad to see a man sae happy,
E'en drown'd himsel amang the nappy.
As bees flee hame wi' lades o' treasure,
The minutes wing'd their way wi' pleasure:
Kings may be blest but Tam was glorious,
O'er a' the ills o' life victorious!

Tam o' Shanter

75

Peter Mackenzie

The Twal' Hours

Peter Mackenzie was one of the leaders of the reform movement
in early nineteenth-century Glasgow. His *Reminiscences of Glasgow
and the West of Scotland*, written in his old age in 1865, provide
fascinating details of the social, economic and political life in the
city during his lifetime.

It was the rule of the Bank in those days to close its doors between the
hours of twelve and one o'clock, to afford the officials time to look over
their forenoon's transactions, to see that all was right, and to prepare
leisurely for the business of the afternoon. This was what was called
the 'twal' hours.' Precisely at one, the doors of the Bank were again
thrown open by John, the old coachman of Mr Carrick, for the miser
really kept a cranking vehicle of that kind. John also acted as the Bank
porter, and by him the doors were again finally closed for the business
of the day, exactly at three. That old man, the porter, had also been
the sort of butler and faithful servant in other respects, of Mr Carrick,
for the long period of nearly fifty years; and when the millionaire died,
it was confidently expected that poor old John would have been noticed
handsomely in his settlement. He left him not a farthing – not even the
gratuity of one year's wages – and all poor *coachie* got was some old
clothes which had been worn almost threadbare by the great Banker,
but miserable man, consisting of corduroy breeches, rig-and-fur worsted
stockings, old spats, without buttons, and one or two old black coats,
and shabby hats of the coarsest brim. In the foregoing numerous ca-
pacities, old John became a real Glasgow character. He knew every
merchant and manufacturer in the city, and could tell all about them,
with their kith and kin, to the bargain. He remembered and conversed
with the great Virginia lords, when they walked towering in their pride
of place, with their scarlet mantles, in the Trongate. He had carried in
his arms, when he was an infant, the illustrious Sir John Moore, the
hero of Corunna, born in this city, to whom Mr Carrick was distantly
related; and poor old John used to tell us many interesting stories about
Glasgow matters when we visited him in the Town's Hospital, many
years ago, where he was enrolled as a pauper, and died; but he was

always polite, and possessed a heart and disposition infinitely more agreeable than that of his great rich worldly master.

Those 'twal' hours,' in particular, were indeed glad moments to old Mr John Marshall, the accountant of the 'Ship;' for, when he got his summations accomplished, which he generally did in the space of a few minutes, he took staff in hand, and toddled over to Archie Ferguson's tavern, at the head of the Stockwell, where he spent the remainder of the hour greatly to his heart's content. He had his glass, and sometimes his pint of rum, his lemons, and his limes. No whisky, or at least little of it, was tasted in those days, by the good people of Glasgow – all fine Jamaica rum – rum punch, and rum toddy, and for many years *rum* was the great liquor trade in Glasgow. We heard the late Mr Wallace of Kelly say, that in early life his father derived upwards of £20,000 per annum alone, from his Rum Plantations in Jamaica, but when rum went out of fashion, and whisky became the order of the day, these rum plantations dwindled almost to nothing. But to our tale. On one occasion, but there were many occasions, we think, we see old Accountant Marshall coming statelily erect from Ferguson's tavern to the Bank's head-quarters. It was a summer day. The rum punch had settled in his head. He was fully six feet in his shoes and buckles, his personage lean and spare. He was venerable, however, for his years, and his powdered hair and silken tie, which gracefully curled almost down to the middle of his back, made him a most striking character at that period in Glasgow. His dress was not less remarkable. It may astonish the youths of the present day to be told of it. He had nankeen breeches, for be it observed, nankeen was fashionable for the old as well as the young, in the days of George the Third. Nankeen trousers and nankeen vests and jackets predominated for many seasons, and our aged hero appreciated them in his own person. Draped out in his nankeens, with white silken stockings on his spindle shanks, a white vest, with its flapping outside pockets, which came farther down than we need describe; a dark claret coat, which reached to his heels, while the neck of it for thickness might have made a good bolster for any child, and with a proboscis for the largest quantity of snuff, our hero, for he was in truth a quiet man, proceeded to take up his wonted position in the Bank chambers. To do so, he behoved to walk through the dark lobby. He staggered to the left side, and held by the wall, and perceiving him in this rather awkward position, one of the youngsters connected with the Bank, offered to guide him to his stool, and in the most affectionate manner, said – 'Hae, Mr Marshall, hold your head, and open your mouth, till I put a peppermint lozenger in it, that will keep the smell of the rum from the nose of Robin;' meaning Mr Carrick. This was not unlike the position of Mr Samuel Hunter's clerk, already noticed. At that moment, it happened that Robin was keeking out of one of the apartments close at hand, and overheard the corollary. He saw how the land lay, at once. His anger was great. The body of the little man, round and portly as it was, quivered with rage. 'You'll no deceive me with your peppermints any longer – pretending to go for your *twal' hours*, and coming back in this manner, reeling and stoving with rum, and bringing discredit on yourself and disparagement on the Bank. If you want to slocken your drouth, Mr Marshall, at twelve o'clock, you must just be contented to step out to the pump-well at the back Court; but never let me see you sooking peppermints, and reeking wi' rum ony mair, in this Bank, at your peril.' This finished the 'twal' hours.'

Reminiscences of Glasgow and the West of Scotland

W.S. Graham

What Will You Have?

William Sydney Graham (1918−86) was born in Greenock. His best-known volume is *The Night Fishing* (1955). His *Collected Poems 1942−1977* appeared in 1979. Graham spent some years in St Ives, Cornwall, which had both an artists' community and a fishing population. Graham was involved in both, and fished himself. This is from the seventh of seven verse letters he wrote trying to establish a relationship between himself and the St Ives characters.

Calum, what will you have?
I'll call the rounds. Remember,
When we fished out of Kinmore
They made their own at the farm.
We drank it dripping hot
Out of an antique worm.
Now, Calum, here's to the keel.
Lift up your drinking arm.
I've waited so long for this,
To meet you in the eye
And in the ear. And now
All time's within our reach.
Drink and these words unperish
Us under the golden drench.

Welcome my dear as heir
To yes again the long
Song of the thorough keel
Moving us through the pitch
Of night in a half gale.
Here at the gunwale farewell
Gives us away this homeward
Night keeled into the final
Breathless element.
Always surely your bent
Is mine. Always surely

My thoroughfare is you.
And that is you by both
The high helmet of light
And by the beast rearing
To sire in the dark kiln.
Watch as you go. Hold
The mizzen there as the sea's
Branches burn and emblazon
Our death under every eye
And burn us into the brain
Of silence in these words.

Letter VII

John Galt

The Town Drummer

John Galt (1779–1839) is best known for his novels, in which
he rendered with shrewdness, humour and irony the vagaries
of human nature as they were affected by social and economic
changes of the late eighteenth century. He is concerned essentially with his native Ayrshire. *The Provost*, from which the following is an extract, is set in 'Gudetown', which is the Ayrshire
town of Irvine.

For many a year one Robin Boss had been town drummer: he was a
relic of some American-war fencibles, and was, to say the God's truth
of him, a divor body, with no manner of conduct, saving a very earnest
endeavour to fill himself fou as often as he could get the means; the
consequence of which was that his face was as plooky as a curran' bun,
and his nose as red as a partan's tae.

One afternoon there was a need to send out a proclamation to abolish
a practice that was growing into a custom, in some of the by-parts of
the town, of keeping swine at large, – ordering them to be confined in
proper styes, and other suitable places. As on all occasions when the
matter to be proclaimed was from the magistrates, Thomas, on this,
was attended by the town-officers in their Sunday garbs, and with their
halberts in their hands; but the abominable and irreverent creature was
so drunk that he wamblet to and fro over the drum, as if there had not
been a bane in his body. He was seemingly as soople and as senseless
as a bolster.

Still, as this was no new thing with him, it might have passed; for
James Hound, the senior officer, was in the practice, when Robin was
in that state, of reading the proclamations himself. On this occasion,
however, James happened to be absent on some hue and cry quest,
and another of the officers (I forget which) was appointed to perform
for him. Robin, accustomed to James, no sooner heard the other man
begin to read than he began to curse and swear at him as an incapable
nincompoop – an impertinent term that he was much addicted to. The
grammar school was at the time skailing and the boys seeing the stramash, gathered round the officer, and yelling and shouting, encouraged
Robin more and more into rebellion, till at last they worked up his

corruption to such a pitch, that he took the drum from about his neck, and made it fly like a bombshell at the officer's head.

The officers behaved very well, for they dragged Robin by the lug and the horn to the Tolbooth, and then came with their complaint to me. Seeing how the authorities had been set at nought, and the necessity there was of making an example, I forthwith ordered Robin to be cashiered from the service of the town; and as so important a concern as a proclamation ought not to be delayed, I likewise, upon the spot, ordered the officers to take a lad that had been also a drummer in a marching regiment, and go with him to make the proclamation.

Nothing could be done in a more earnest and zealous public spirit than this was done by me. But habit had begot in the town a partiality for the drunken ne'er-do-well, Robin; and this just act of mine was immediately condemned as a daring stretch of arbitrary power, and the consequence was that when the council met next day some sharp words flew among us, as to my usurping an undue authority, and the thank I got for my pains was the mortification to see the worthless body restored to full power and dignity, with no other reward than an admonition to behave better for the future. Now, I leave it to the unbiassed judgment of posterity to determine if any public man could be more ungraciously treated by his colleagues than I was on this occasion. But, verily, the council had their reward.

The divor, Robin Boss, being, as I have recorded, reinstated in office, soon began to play his old tricks. In the course of the week after the Michaelmas term at which my second provostry ended, he was so insupportably drunk that he fell head foremost into his drum, which cost the town five-and-twenty shillings for a new one – an accident that was not without some satisfaction to me; and I trow I was not sparing in my derisive commendations on the worth of such a public officer. Nevertheless, he was still kept on, some befriending him for compassion, and others as it were to spite me.

But Robin's good behaviour did not end with breaking the drum, and costing a new one. In the course of the winter it was his custom to beat, 'Go to bed, Tom,' about ten o'clock at night, and the *réveille* at five in the morning. In one of his drunken fits he made a mistake, and instead of going his rounds as usual at ten o'clock, he had fallen asleep in a change-house, and, waking about the midnight hour in the terror of some whisky dream, he seized his drum, and running into the streets, began to strike the fire-beat in the most awful manner.

It was a fine clear frosty moonlight, and the hollow sound of the drum resounded through the silent streets like thunder. In a moment everybody was a-foot, and the cry of 'Whar is't? whar's the fire?' was heard echoing from all sides. Robin, quite unconscious that he alone was the cause of the alarm, still went along beating the dreadful summons. I heard the noise and rose; but while I was drawing on my stockings, in the chair at the bed-head, and telling Mrs Pawkie to compose herself, for our houses were all insured, I suddenly recollected that Robin had the night before neglected to go his rounds at ten o'clock as usual, and the thought came into my head that the alarm might be one of his inebriated mistakes. So, instead of dressing myself any further, I went to the window, and looked out through the glass, without opening it, for, being in my night-clothes, I was afraid of taking cold.

The street was as throng as on a market-day, and every face in the moonlight was pale with fear. Men and lads were running with their coats, and carrying their breeches in their hands; wives and maidens were all asking questions at one another, and even lasses were fleeing to and fro, like water nymphs with urns, having stoups and pails in their hands. There was swearing and tearing of men, hoarse with the rage of impatience, at the Tolbooth, getting out the fire-engine from its stance under the stair; and loud and terrible afar off, and over all, came the peal of alarm from drunken Robin's drum.

I could scarcely keep my composity when I beheld and heard all this, for I was soon thoroughly persuaded of the fact. At last I saw Deacon Girdwood, the chief advocate and champion of Robin, passing down the causey like a demented man, with a red nightcap, and his big-coat on – for some had cried that the fire was in his yard.

'Deacon,' cried I, opening the window, forgetting in the jocularity of the moment the risk I ran from being so naked, 'whar away sae fast, deacon?'

The deacon stopped and said, 'Is't out? is't out?'

'Gang your ways home,' quo' I very coolly, 'for I hae a notion that a' this hobleshow's but the fume of a gill in your friend Robin's head.'

'It's no possible!' exclaimed the deacon.

'Possible here or possible there, Mr Girdwood,' quo' I, 'it's oure cauld for me to stand talking wi' you here; we'll learn the rights o't in the morning; so, good-night;' and with that I pulled down the window.

But scarcely had I done so when a shout of laughter came gathering up the street, and soon after poor drunken Robin was brought along by the cuff of the neck, between two of the town-officers, one of them carrying his drum. The next day he was put out of office for ever, and folk recollecting in what manner I had acted towards him before, the outcry about my arbitrary power was forgotten in the blame that was heaped upon those who had espoused Robin's cause against me.

The Provost

Immense Quantities of Whisky

The *Statistical Account of Scotland* was a massive work in twenty-one volumes edited by Sir John Sinclair and published between 1791 and 1799. It contained an account of the social and economic situation of every parish in Scotland, written by the parish minister. It is thus an invaluable source of information for the social historian.

Of the People. – It has been frequently observed, the inhabitants of the parish of Scone were distinguished only by the decency of their dress and appearance, the propriety of their manners and behaviour. The fact may be accounted for, in part, from the example of the family of Stormont, who were patterns of religion and good morals as well as decorous manners; and in part, from the powerful ministry of a very worthy man, who was a long time their pastor; causes, which, in a greater or less

degree, will always influence the morals of the people. The general character of the present race is sobriety, industry, and economy. The lower class are humane, civil, obliging, and hospitable. The rich are more: They are genteel, and well bred. But the best proof of their morals is, that most of them are in comfortable, and many of them in affluent circumstances, according to their rank in life; and that no instance can be remembered, in which any persons of this parish suffered the punishment of crimes.

The public houses, simply as such, would not, it is presumed, have any bad influence on the morals of the people, were it not for the immense quantities of whisky which they retail, in place of well-made ale, which was formerly the only beverage. There are men in this part of the country, who consider the large distilleries as gulphs, which swallow up prodigious quantities of grain, and discharge nothing but what serves to destroy the health and morals of the people; and they very much desire that the legislature would devise some way, which, seconded by the example of the great, should bring again into fashion the use of home-made fermented malt liquors, which the encouragement given to the distilleries has brought almost entirely into disuse.

Statistical Account of Scotland, XVIII
(Parish of Scone, County of Perth), 1796

Robert Henryson

The Poet's Comfort

These verses are from the opening of Henryson's great narrative poem, where he describes how he makes himself comfortable by the fire with a drink before he starts to compose his sequel to Chaucer's *Troilus and Cresseid*.

And doolie sessoun to one cairful dyte
Suld correspond and be equivalent:
Rich sa it was quhen I began to wryte
This tragedie – the wedder richt fervent,
Quhen Aries, in middis of the Lent,
Schouris of haill gart fra the north discend,
That scantlie fra the cauld I micht defend...

I mend the fyre and beikit me about,
Than tuik ane drink my spreitis to comfort,
And armit me weill fra the cauld thairout,
To cut the winter nicht and mak it schort,
I tuik ane quair – and left all uther sport –
Writtin by worthie Chaucer glorious,
Of fair Creisseid and worthie Troylus.

Sydney Goodsir Smith

Song: The Steeple Bar, Perth

Sydney Goodsir Smith (1915–75), one of the finest of the second
generation (after MacDiarmid) of poets who wrote in Scots, was a
notable drinker and good companion. As well as publishing several
volumes of poetry, he edited a number of books on aspects of
Scottish literature.

O it's dowf tae be drinkin alane, my luve,
   When I wud drink wi my dear,
Nor Crabbie nor Bell's can fire me, luve,
   As they wud an you were here.

O I'd drink wi us aa again, my luve,
   As we aa did yester year,
But me buckos 're scattered afar, my luve,
   An I greit intil my beer.

Wi my third I'll drink tae oor Denis, luve,
   My fourth great John's, the bauld an steir,
My fifth auld Hector's, the rebelly carle,
   An my sixth tae oorsels, my dear.

And noo I've forgot dear Bonz the mad –
   Wud the Pawky Duke were near,
So he'll hae the seeventh, the darlin lad,
   And again tae oorsels, my dear.

My brains 're fleein, I cannae think
   O' the dizzen ithers I wud were here;
Tae Maury the neist wee Bell's I'll drink,
   Tae Dauvit a pint – an I'm sunk – gey near.

O I'm gettin awee thing fou, my luve,
   An donnert an like tae fleer –
For, jeez, it's dreich tae get pissed, my luve,
   Wi nane o my looed yins here.

John Strang

The Meridian Club

The full title of Strang's book, from which this extract is taken, in *Glasgow and its Clubs; or Glimpses of the Conditions, Manners, Characters, Oddities of the City during the Past & Present Century, by John Strang LL.D.* It was published in 1856, and provides exactly the kind of information we would expect from its title.

Considerate reader! if thou has ever wandered from the *Cross* of Glasgow to its *Westergate*, before that portion of the City had attained the ducal appellation of Argyle-street, which it now bears, then mightest thou remember to have seen, on leaving the Trongate, an old dingy square building, two stories in height, with small dirty windows, and having two doors, one in front and one behind. At the back of this gloomy mansion, and within a wall, there was a piece of vacant ground bearing one or two stunted trees, and generally occupied by a large haystack. Within the domain itself, now many years removed, it may be truly said that, during the progress of at least half a century, many a happy or painful moment was experienced in the breast of the active and bustling individuals who daily frequented it. It was in fact here that the oldest banking establishment connected with Glasgow was located, on its removal, about 1776, from the Bridgegate, where it was first fixed in 1750. In the street floor of the tenement, formerly the western wing of the Shawfield mansion, all its monetary transactions were carried on; and in the flat above, the head and regulator of its weighty affairs lived and died. The banking-house to which we allude, it is perhaps almost unnecessary to state, was that known as 'the Ship,' and the business was carried on under the firm of Carrick, Brown, & Co. The notes which the Company issued were printed partly in blue and partly in black ink, and sported on their face the figure of a vessel in full sail; and being partly *Guinea* notes, were far more greedily taken, throughout all parts of the West of Scotland, than were even the golden effigiæ of George III on the coin of the same value.

As this was the first bank that in boyhood we had entered, the impression which that and hundreds of successive visits made on our memory can never be forgotten. We distinctly see before us the dark passage which led into the principal business room, where the cash for cheques or discounted bills was given – the high wooden partition, with its rail and screen, which separated the banking officials from the public – the old desk, of common wood, covered with dirty leather, in which were placed the various notes – the constant motion to which the hinges of this receptacle of money were subjected by the active cashier, whose head was ever and anon required to support the uplifted lid – the slow and solemn enumeration of names by the tall pig-tailed accountant – the cantankerous-looking countenance of the individual who received payment of the bills, and who, with some others, occupied an equally dingy apartment on the south side of the building. We can never likewise forget the small chamber assigned to the then manager himself, well known by the epithet of the 'sweating-room,' where, seated on a wooden-legged stool, at a high desk, he received all his customers with the greatest coolness and politeness; and when even declining to discount a bill, he ever did so with a courteous smile, and with the never-to-be-forgotten saying – 'It's not convenient', which saying, when once uttered, was never to be recalled. What a striking contrast does such a state of things afford to the present day – to the gorgeous telling-rooms of our modern banks, and the administrative superiority of our modern officials!

We have been more particular than perhaps may be considered necessary in describing this establishment of former days, from the circumstance that it was to the peculiar tastes and habits of certain of its officials that Glasgow owed the rise of her MERIDIAN CLUB. The fact is, it had been the custom of the Ship Bank, since its first establishment, to shut its doors between the hours of one and two o'clock – that being the then universal time for dinner in the City; and hence, during that space of time at least, every one connected with it was allowed to go where or to do what best pleased his fancy. While, therefore, the more youthful and sedate dedicated the idle hour to a walk or some other sober occupation, it was the daily duty of certain of the older and more singular to join a squad of carbuncle-faced worthies, who regularly met in a back parlour of a house in Stockwell-street, for a long time famous for the excellence of its trade and its tipple. The members of this fraternity were all such sworn friends of John Barleycorn, that although it was held by the majority of mankind, even at that drinking period, to be not altogether *en regle* to *call* for him before dinner, they, in spite of the fashion, made it an invariable rule to shake hands with that soother of humanity as nearly at noon as possible. The appellation of the *Meridian*, which was happily made choice of as the sign of their union, will appear as appropriate as it was descriptive, when it is recollected that some of the brotherhood were even busy in their vocation of taking *spiritual* comfort ere the sun had attained to 'high meridian;' and what is more, many of them had a bottle under their belt, and a bee in their bonnet,

89

long before the hour at which modern exquisites conceive that the day can possibly be sufficiently well *aired* for sunning themselves on the *pave*!

The sittings of this Club, although daily held, were never known to be on any occasion either long or noisy. The individuals, indeed, who composed the Meridian, assembled not to speak but to swallow; a can and not conversation was their object; the greatest extent of their loquacity being rarely carried beyond a 'Here goes!' and a 'Here goes again!' The fact was, this whisky-bolting divan, being business men, never dreamed of occupying the club-room for more than an hour, or of spending more time than was absolutely necessary for clearing their throats or soothing the irritated coats of their stomach. We shall never forget the slender six feet nucleus of this knot of forenoon topers – his prismatic proboscis, planted on a cadaverous countenance, and the leering look of his small twinkling eye when any handsome form or pretty face by hazard crossed his path, when wending his way from the bank to the club-room; neither can we forget the mode which he pursued for concealing his *Meridian* manners from the olfactory nerves of his staid and sober employers. As the clock struck one, it was quite certain that down from the bank the member ran to join his already assembled *cordial* companions. And as the sittings of the fraternity were so short, and his business *sanctum* so near, there was no difficulty in performing all the duties of a member of the Meridian within the limited term of its daily sederunt. The only difficulty, in fact, he experienced, was how he might best kill the flavour of the Ferintosh, which, he well knew, was little less than poison to the populace before one o'clock, although felt to be palatable and medicinal after four. He thought of many modes of sweetening his stomach's tell-tale zephyr, and at last, for that special purpose, hit upon a specific equal to the most potent lozenges which any modern Butler has since invented. Delighted with the discovery, he felt determined one day, on returning from Stockwell, to communicate the valuable secret to another equally Meridian-minded banking-house brother. Armed, therefore, with the required specific in his hand, and a goodly portion of it in his stomach, the copper-nosed member slipped into what was emphatically designated 'the other room,' and stealing behind a blue-coated character, occupying the place of his bottle companion, he gave him a hearty slap on the back, and presenting the specific, cried out, with joyful satisfaction, 'Here, my old cock, is one of Robin's deceivers for you!' The hawk-eye which was immediately upturned from gloating over the folios of a gold-telling ledger – of one whom, in verity, it might be said with Spenser, that

> 'His life was nigh unto death's door yplaste;
> And thread-bare cote and cobbled shoes he wore;
> He scarce good morsel all his life did taste,

But both from backe and belly still did spare
To fill his bags, and richesse to compare,
Yet child ne kinsman living, had he none
To leave them to,' –

and who, that day, most unfortunately had wandered, during the inter-
val, from his *sweating* chamber, told the would-be deceiving member of
the Meridian, that he himself was at least in this instance the *deceived*.
Ashamed of having thus, by mistake, *indorsed* the back of his employer
for that of his associate, he would have fain *protested* against his want of
attention, as he was wont to do against that of others; but the 'not convenient' look and bow of his master – for it was really him – stilled him
into silence, and caused him to retire with as sorrowful a heart as ever
fell to the lot of any hapless needy wight, who was doomed to receive the
like hope-blasting answer to a demand for discount. We have frequently
thought what a striking picture this occurrence would have made in the
hands of an Ostade or a Wilkie! The master's short, round, composed-
looking figure, with his keen and scrutinising features, over which flowed
a rather thin crop of greyish hair, tied together behind with a small black
ribbon into a sort of petty pigtail – his coat of dark blue, double-breasted,
and hanging down to his heels – his woollen waistcoat, with broad and
narrow stripes running up and down, and ornamented with pearl buttons – his nether garments, reaching only to his knee – and his limbs
encased in white broad-ribbed stockings, with their extremities planted
in a pair of wide high shoes tied like his hair with a similar black silk
ribbon; before him the open ledger, and all the singular still-life adjuncts
of the curiously-lighted apartment; and next, the servant, with his tall
gaunt form, and face redolent of every colour with which a limner might
dream to *set* his pallet, before beginning to idealise the character of John
Barleycorn himself – his hoary locks, gathered into a heavy club-tie – his
piercing eye and outshot lips when anything excited him, and particularly when the idea of a brimming goblet flitted, either in memory or
anticipation, athwart his brain – his odd-cut coat, shaped as with the
shears of many a bypast age – his straight but slender legs, frequently
'faithless to the fuddled foot,' and protected from cold by worsted hose –
his left hand outstretched, filled with the concentrated essence of *deceit*,
while his upraised right was at the instant falling with all the rapture
of a successful dodge on the shoulder of his unknown master; – what a
glorious speaking group would such a pair have formed! A picture like
this would have required none of that endless *drumming* for support,
which is now-a-days so pertinaciously practised in behalf even of the most
meritorious of modern pictorial efforts. As to the original, we may safely
affirm, that while the banker himself might probably have grudged to
give so much gold for so little canvas, sure are we, that each member of
the Club of which the worthy accountant was the loadstar, would have

91

exerted himself to preserve for posterity so illustrative a record and reminiscence of the Meridian Club. The two individuals of whom we have just been speaking, are now long gone to that 'undiscovered country,' to which the one could not transport his gold, and in which the other will not need to declaim, as was his constant custom, when carrying a glass to his mouth, against the brandy-denying duties of the Excise.

The Meridian Club continued to meet for years even after the demise of its original and most regular member; for verily the mantle of this pig-tailed father of the fraternity most happily fell on the shoulders of an equally worthy pig-tailed character, commonly called the *Sherra*, whose daily devotion to the cause of forenoon potations tended, in a great measure, to keep together, longer probably than modern usages would have permitted, this most remarkable knot of noontide topers. They have all, however, each in his turn, been doomed to drink the last *bottom* of the favourite beverage of the brotherhood. The score, in fact, has been made up, and the reckoning settled. But we must in justice add, that, notwithstanding all which temperance societies and restricted licensing have done to restrain the bibacious propensity of Scotsmen, we believe there are yet, at the present hour, many occasional Meridian Clubs held within this great and growing City – that it is, in fact, still the custom for the craftsman of the town, and the farmer from the country, to imagine that no business can be properly settled except when sealed with the spirit of John Barleycorn. Some of these, we have no doubt, may still be found nestling about the head of Stockwell-street; – but, as a faithful annalist, before closing for ever the door of the singular and long-frequented Meridian Club-room, we must chronicle the melancholy fact, that even the bustling Boniface, who, at the final meeting of the far-famed Meridian, ministered to the members' wants, has likewise reached the goal of all earthly toil and anxiety where the thirsty cease from *fuddling*, and the 'weary are at rest!' From our heart we say of all, *Requiescant in pace!*

Glasgow and its Clubs

Lewis Grassic Gibbon

Chris's Wedding

Gibbon's real name was James Leslie Mitchell (1901–35). This piece comes from *Sunset Song*, the first volume of a trilogy collectively entitled *A Scots Quair*, set mostly in the Howe of the Mearns, Kincardineshire. Chris is the heroine, in some ways a symbol of modern Scottish rural history.

Then they all drank up again, and God knows who mightn't have made the next speech if Chae then hadn't stood up and cried *The night's near on us. Who's game for a daylight dance at Chris's wedding?*

So out they all went to the kitchen, it was cold enough there from the heat of the room, but nothing to the cold rife air of the barn when the first of them had crossed the close and stood in the door. But Mistress Melon had kindled a brazier with coal, it crackled fine, well away from the straw, Rob tuned up his fiddle, Chae squeaked on his melodeon, it began to feel brisk and warm even while you stood and near shivered your sark off. Chris was there with the men, of course, and the children and Mistress Gordon and Mistress Mutch and Mistress Strachan were there, Mistress Munro had stayed behind to help clear the tables, she said, and some whispered it was more than likely she'd clear most of the clearings down her own throat, by God she couldn't have eaten a mouthful since Candlemas.

But then Chae cried *Strip the Willow*, and they all lined up, and the melodeon played bonnily in Chae's hands, and Long Rob's fiddle-bow was darting and glimmering, and in two minutes in the whirl and go of *Strip the Willow*, there wasn't a cold soul in Blawearie barn, or a cold sole either. Then here, soon's they'd finished, was Mistress Melon with a great jar of hot toddy to drink, she set it on a bench between Chae and Long Rob. And whoever wanted to drink had just to go there, few were bashful in the going, too; and another dance started, it was a schottische, and Chris found herself in the arms of the minister, he could dance like a daft young lad. And as he swung her round and around he opened his mouth and cried *Hooch!* and so did the red Highlander, McIvor, *Hooch!* careering by with fat Kirsty Strachan, real scared-like she looked, clipped round the waist.

93

Then Chae and Long Rob hardly gave them a breather, they were at it dance on dance; and every time they stopped for a panting second Chae would dip in the jar and give Rob a wink and cry *Here's to you, man!* and Rob would dip, solemn-like as well, and say *Same to you!* and off the fiddle and melodeon would go again, faster than ever. Ewan danced the schottische with prim Mistress Gordon, but for waltzing he found a quean from the Mains, a red-faced, daft-like limmer, she screamed with excitement and everybody laughed, Chris laughed as well. Some were watching to see if she did, she knew, and she heard a whisper she'd have all her work cut out looking after him, coarse among the queans he was, Ewan Tavendale. But she didn't care, she knew it a lie, Ewan was hers and hers only but she wished he would dance with her for a change. And here at the *Petronella* he was, he anyway hadn't been drinking, in the noise of the dance as they swayed up and down the barn he whispered *Well, Chris?* and she whispered back *Fine,* and he said *You're the bonniest thing ever seen in Kinraddie, Long Rob was right.* And she said she liked him to think so, and he called her back in the darkness away from the dancers, and kissed her quickly and slowly, she didn't hurry either, it was blithe and glad to stand there kissing, each strained to hear when they'd be discovered.

And then they were, Chae crying *Where's the bride and the groom? Damn't it, they're lost!* and out they'd to come. Chae cried was there anyone else could play the melodeon? and young Jock Gordon cried back

to him *Ay, fine that*, and came stitering across the floor and sat himself down by the toddy jar, and played loud and clear and fine. Then Chae caught Chris, he said to Ewan *Away, you greedy brute, wait a while till she's yours forever and aye*, and he danced right neatly, you didn't expect it from Chae, with his grey eyes laughing down at you. And as he danced he said suddenly, grave-like, *Never doubt your Ewan, Chris, or never let him know that you do. That's the hell of a married life. Praise him up and tell him he's fine, that there's not a soul in the Howe can stand beside him, and he'll want to cuddle you till the day he dies; and he'll blush at the sight of you fifty years on as much as he does the day.* She said *I'll try*, and *Thank you, Chae*, and he said *Och, it must be the whisky speaking*, and surrendered her up to Ellison, and took the melodeon from Gordon again, but staggered and leant back against the sack that hung as a draught-shield behind the musician's place. Down came the sack and there among the hay was the minister and the maid from the Mains that had scraiched so loud, she'd her arms round him and the big curly bull was kissing the quean like a dog lapping up its porridge.

Chris's heart near stopped, but Chae snatched up the sack, hooked it back on its hook again, nobody saw the sight except himself and Chris and maybe Long Rob. But you couldn't be sure about Rob, he looked as solemn as five owls all in one, and was playing as though, said Chae, he was paid by piece-work and not by time.

So they closed the door of the stable and went into their supper, everybody ate near as well as at tea-time; fair starved they were with the dancing and drink. Chris had thought she herself was tired till she ate some supper, and then she felt as fresh as ever, and backed up Long Rob, who looked twice as sober as any of the men and had drunk about twice as much as any three of them, when he cried *Who's for a dance again?* Mistress Melon had the toddy-jar filled fresh full and they carried that out, everybody came to the barn this time except Mistress Munro, *No, no, I'll clear the table.*

And then the fun slackened off, the barn was warm, folk sat or lay on the benches or straw, Chris looked round and saw nothing of the minister then, maybe he'd gone. She whispered to Chae about that, but he said *Damn the fears, he's out to be sick, can't you hear him like a cat with a fish-bone in its throat?* And hear him they could, but Chris had been right after all, he didn't come back. Maybe he was shamed and maybe he just lost his way, for next noon there were folk who swore they'd seen the marks of great feet that walked round and round in a circle, circle after circle, all across the parks from Blawearie to the Manse; and if these weren't the minister's feet they must have been the devil's, you could choose whichever you liked.

Sunset Song

95

Hugh MacDiarmid

Old Wife in High Spirits

In an Edinburgh Pub

Hugh MacDiarmid was the pseudonym of Christopher Murray
Grieve 1892−1978, Scotland's greatest modern poet and one of the
greatest of any time. His revival of Scots as a language for poetry,
in which he used words from older Scottish literature as well as
from the vernacular of his own time, has had a marked influence
on younger Scottish poets. His relish of life lived with genuineness
and abandon is given fine expression in this poem.

An auld wumman cam' in, a mere rickle o' banes, in a faded black dress
And a bonnet wi' beads o' jet rattlin' on it;
A puir-lookin' cratur, you'd think she could haurdly ha'e had less
Life left in her and still lived, but dagonit!

He gied her a stiff whisky – she was nervous as a troot
And could haurdly haud the tumbler, puir cratur;
Syne he gied her anither, joked wi' her, and anither, and syne
Wild as the whisky up cam' her nature.

The rod that struck water frae the rock in the desert
Was naething to the life that sprang oot o' her;
The dowie auld soul was twinklin' and fizzin' wi' fire;
You never saw ocht sae souple and kir.

Like a sackful o' monkeys she was, and her lauchin'
Loupit up whiles to incredible heights;
Wi' ane owre the eight her temper changed and her tongue
Flew juist as the forkt lichtnin' skites.

The heich skeich auld cat was fair in her element;
Wanton as a whirlwind, and shairly better that way
Than a' crippen thegither wi' laneliness and cauld
Like a foretaste o' the graveyaird clay.

96

Some folk nae doot'll condemn gie'in' a guid spree
To the puir dune body and raither she endit her days
Like some auld tashed copy o' the Bible yin sees
On a street book-barrow's tipenny trays,

A' I ken is weel-fed and weel-put-on though they be
Ninety per cent o' respectable folk never hae
As muckle life in their creeshy carcases frae beginnin' to end
As kythed in that wild auld carline that day!

Remarkable Moderation

Distilleries, Alehouses, &c. – There are 2 licensed stills of 30 gallons each in the parish, and 24 licensed retailers of ale, beer, and other exciseable liquors. The number of distillers and retailers may be considered as a circumstance unfavourable to the health, and the morals of the people. However, it cannot be said, that the people are addicted to drinking. Even at weddings, and on holidays, instances of persons drinking to excess are few, and a drunken squabble is extremely rare. It is somewhat remarkable, that among people who hardly know how to make a bargain, or pay a debt, except over a dram of whisky, moderation should be so generally observed; particularly when it is considered, that at the fairs, every house, hut, and shed in the respective villages, is converted into a dram-shop.

Statistical Account of Scotland, V
(Parish of Moulin, County of Perth), 1793.

George Douglas

Social Drinking

The full name of the author was George Douglas Brown (1869—1902). *The House with the Green Shutters* (1901), whence this extract comes, is a bitter counterblast to the sentimentalising 'Kailyard' novels of Scottish village life and in its grim critical pessimism marked a new movement in Scottish literature.

There were two things to be said against Allan, and two only – unless, of course, you consider drink an objection. Wit with him was less the moment's glittering flash than the anecdotal bang; it was a fine old crusted blend which he stored in the cellars of his mind to bring forth on suitable occasions, as cob-webby as his wine. And it tickled his vanity to have a crowd of admiring youngsters round him to whom he might retail his anecdotes, and play the brilliant *raconteur*. He had cronies of his own years, and he was lordly and jovial amongst them – yet he wanted another *entourage*. He was one of those middle-aged bachelors who like a train of youngsters behind them, whom they favour in return for homage. The wealthy man who had been a peasant lad delighted to act the jovial host to sons of petty magnates from his home. Batch after batch as they came up to College were drawn around him – partly because their homage pleased him, and partly because he loved anything whatever that came out of Barbie. There was no harm in Allan – though when his face was in repose you saw the look in his eye at times of a man defrauding his soul. A robustious young fellow of sense and brains would have found in this lover of books and a bottle not a bad comrade. But he was the worst of cronies for a weak swaggerer like Gourlay. For Gourlay, admiring the older man's jovial power, was led on to imitate his faults, to think them virtues and a credit; and he lacked the clear, cool head that kept Allan's faults from flying away with him.

At dinner that night there were several braw, braw lads of Barbie Water. There were Tarmillan the doctor (a son of Irrendavie), Logan the cashier, Tozer the Englishman, old Partan – a guileless and inquiring mind – and half a dozen students raw from the west. The students were of the kind that goes up to College with the hayseed sticking in its hair. Two are in a Colonial Cabinet now, two are in the poorhouse. So they go.

Tarmillan was the last to arrive. He came in sucking his thumb, into which he had driven a splinter while conducting an experiment.

'I've a morbid horror of lockjaw,' he explained. 'I never get a jag from a pin but I see myself in the shape of a hoop, semicircular, with my head on one end of a table, my heels on the other, and a doctor standing on my navel trying to reduce the curvature.'

'Gosh!' said Partan, who was a literal fool, 'is that the treatment they purshoo?'

'That's the treatment!' said Tarmillan, sizing up his man. 'Oh, it's a queer thing lockjaw! I remember when I was gold-mining in Tibet, one of our carriers who died of lockjaw had such a circumbendibus in his body that we froze him and made him the hoop of a bucket to carry our water in. You see he was a thin bit man, and iron was scarce.'

'Ay, man!' cried Partan, 'you've been in Tibet?'

'Often,' waved Tarmillan, 'often! I used to go there every summer.'

Partan, who liked to extend his geographical knowledge, would have talked of Tibet for the rest of the evening – and Tarmie would have told him news – but Allan broke in.

'How's the book, Tarmillan?' he inquired.

Tarmillan was engaged on a treatise which those who are competent to judge consider the best thing of its kind ever written.

'Oh, don't ask me,' he writhed. 'Man, it's an irksome thing to write, and to be asked about it makes you squirm. It's almost as offensive to ask a man when his book will be out as to ask a woman when she'll be delivered. I'm glad you invited me – to get away from the confounded thing. It's become a blasted tyrant. A big work's a mistake; it's a monster that devours the brain. I neglect my other work for that fellow of mine; he bags everything I think. I never light on a new thing, but "Hullo!" I cry, "here's an idea for the book!" If you are engaged on a big subject, all your thinking works into it or out of it.'

'M'yes,' said Logan; 'but that's a swashing way of putting it.'

'It's the danger of the aphorism,' said Allan, 'that it states too much in trying to be small. – Tozer, what do you think?'

'I never was engaged on a big subject,' sniffed Tozer.

'We're aware o' that!' said Tarmillan.

Tozer went under, and Tarmillan had the table. Allan was proud of him.

'Courage is the great thing,' said he. 'It often succeeds by the mere show of it. It's the timid man that a dog bites. Run *at* him and he runs.'

He was speaking to himself rather than the table, admiring the courage that had snubbed Tozer with a word. But his musing remark rang a bell in young Gourlay. By Jove, he had thought that himself, so he had! He was a hollow thing, he knew, but a buckram pretence prevented the world from piercing to his hollowness. The son of his courageous sire (whom he equally admired and feared) had learned to play the game of

100

bluff. A bold front was half the battle. He had worked out his little theory, and it was with a shock of pleasure the timid youngster heard great Allan give it forth. He burned to let him know that he had thought that too.

To the youngsters, fat of face and fluffy of its circling down, the talk was a banquet of the gods. For the first time in their lives they heard ideas (such as they were) flung round them royally. They yearned to show that they were thinkers too. And Gourlay was fired with the rest.

'I heard a very good one the other day from old Bauldy Johnston,' said Allan, opening his usual wallet of stories when the dinner was in full swing. At a certain stage of the evening 'I heard a good one' was the invariable keynote of his talk. If you displayed no wish to hear the 'good one,' he was huffed. 'Bauldy was up in Edinburgh,' he went on, 'and I met him near the Scott Monument and took him to Lockhart's for a dram. You remember what a friend he used to be of old Will Overton. I wasn't aware, by-the-bye, that Will was dead till Bauldy told me, *"He was a great fellow my friend Will,"* he rang out in yon deep voice of his. *"The thumb-mark of his Maker was wet in the clay of him."* Man, it made a quiver go down my spine.'

'Oh, Bauldy has been a kenned phrase-maker for the last forty year,' said Tarmillan. 'But every other Scots peasant has the gift. To hear Englishmen talk, you would think Carlyle was unique for the word that sends the picture home – they give the man the credit of his race. But I've heard fifty things better than 'willowy man' in the stable a-hame on a wat day in hairst – fifty things better – from men just sitting on the cornkists and chowing beans.'

'I know a better one than that,' said Allan. Tarmillan had told no story, you observe, but Allan was so accustomed to saying 'I know a better one than that,' that it escaped him before he was aware. 'I remember when Bauldy went off to Paris on the spree. He kept his mouth shut when he came back, for he was rather ashamed o' the outburst. But the bodies were keen to hear. "What's the incense like in Notre Dame?" said Johnny Coe, with his een big. *"Burning stink!"* said Bauldy.'

'I can cap that with a better one still,' said Tarmillan, who wasn't to be done by any man. 'I was with Bauldy when he quarrelled Tam Gibb of Hoochan-doe. Hoochan-doe's a yelling ass, and he threatened Bauldy – oh, he would do this, and he would do that, and he would do the other thing. *"Damn ye, would ye threaten me?"* cried Bauldy. *"I'll gar your brains jaup red to the heavens!"* And I 'clare to God, sirs, a nervous man looked up to see if the clouds werena spattered with the gore!'

Tozer cleared a sarcastic windpipe.

'Why do you clear your throat like that?' said Tarmillan – 'like a craw with the croup, on a bare branch against a gray sky in November! If I had a throat like yours, I'd cut it and be done wi't.'

'I wonder what's the cause of that extraordinary vividness in the speech of the Scotch peasantry?' said Allan – more to keep the blades from bickering than from any wish to know.

'It comes from a power of seeing things vividly inside your mind,' said a voice, timorous and wheezy, away down the table.

What cockerel was this crowing?

They turned, and beheld the blushing Gourlay.

But Tarmillan and Tozer were at it again, and he was snubbed. Jimmy Wilson sniggered, and the other youngsters enjoyed his discomfiture. Huh! What right has *he* to set up his pipe?

His shirt stuck to his back. He would have liked the ground to open and swallow him.

He gulped a huge swill of whisky to cover his vexation; and oh, the mighty difference! A sudden courage flooded his veins. He turned with a scowl on Wilson, and, 'What the devil are *you* sniggering at?' he growled. Logan, the only senior who marked the by-play, thought him a hardy young spunkie.

The moment the whisky had warmed the cockles of his heart Gourlay ceased to care a rap for the sniggerers. Drink deadened his nervous perception of the critics on his right and left, and set him free to follow his idea undisturbed. It was an idea he had long cherished – being one of the few that ever occurred to him. He rarely made phrases himself – though, curiously enough, his father often did without knowing it – the harsh grind of his character producing a flash. But Gourlay was aware of his uncanny gift of visualization – or of 'seeing things in the inside of his head,' as he called it – and vanity prompted the inference, that this was the faculty that sprang the metaphor. His theory was now clear and eloquent before him. He was realizing for the first time in his life (with a sudden joy in the discovery) the effect of whisky to unloose the brain; sentences went hurling through his brain with a fluency that thrilled. If he had the ear of the company, now he had the drink to hearten him, he would show Wilson and the rest that he wasn't such a blasted fool! In a room by himself he would have spouted to the empty air.

Some such point he had reached in the hurrying jumble of his thoughts when Allan addressed him.

Allan did not mean his guest to be snubbed. He was a gentleman at heart, not a cad like Tozer; and this boy was the son of a girl whose laugh he remembered in the gloamings at Tenshillingland.

'I beg your pardon, John,' he said in heavy benevolence – he had reached that stage – 'I beg your pardon. I'm afraid you was interrupted.'

Gourlay felt his heart a lump in his throat, but he rushed into speech.

'Metaphor comes from the power of seeing things in the inside of your head,' said the unconscious disciple of Aristotle – 'seeing them so vivid that you see the likeness between them. When Bauldy Johnston said 'the thumb-mark of his Maker was wet in the clay of him,' he *saw* the print of a thumb in wet clay, and he *saw* the Almighty making a man out of mud, the way He used to do in the Garden of Eden lang syne. So Bauldy flashed the two ideas together, and the metaphor sprang! A man'll never make phrases unless he can see things in the middle of his brain. *I* can see things in the middle of my brain,' he went on cockily – 'anything I want to! I don't need to shut my eyes either. They just come up before me.'

'Man, you're young to have noticed these things, John,' said Jock Allan. 'I never reasoned it out before, but I'm sure you're in the right o't.'

He spoke more warmly than he felt, because Gourlay had flushed and panted and stammered (in spite of inspiring bold John Barleycorn) while airing his little theory, and Allan wanted to cover him. But Gourlay took it as a tribute to his towering mind. Oh, but he was the proud mannikin.

103

'Pass the watter!' he said to Jimmy Wilson, and Jimmy passed it meekly.

Logan took a fancy to Gourlay on the spot. He was a slow, sly, cosy man, with a sideward laugh in his eye, a humid gleam. And because his blood was so genial and so slow, he liked to make up to brisk young fellows, whose wilder outbursts might amuse him. They quickened his sluggish blood. No bad fellow, and good-natured in his heavy way, he was what the Scotch call a 'slug for the drink.' A 'slug for the drink' is a man who soaks and never succumbs. Logan was the more dangerous a crony on that account. Remaining sober while others grew drunk, he was always ready for another dram, always ready with an oily chuckle for the sploring nonsense of his satellites. He would see them home in the small hours, taking no mean advantage over them, never scorning them because they 'couldn't carry it,' only laughing at their daft vagaries. And next day he would gurgle, 'So-and-so was screwed last night, and, man, if you had heard his talk!' Logan had enjoyed it. He hated to drink by himself, and liked a splurging youngster with whom to go the rounds.

He was attracted to Gourlay by the manly way he tossed his drink, and by the false fire it put into him. But he made no immediate advance. He sat smiling in creeshy benevolence, beaming on Gourlay but saying nothing. When the party was ended, however, he made up to him going through the door.

'I'm glad to have met you, Mr Gourlay,' said he. 'Won't you come round to the Howff for a while?'

'The Howff?' said Gourlay.

'Yes,' said Logan; 'haven't ye heard o't? It's a snug bit house where some of the West Country billies forgather for a nicht at e'en. Oh, nothing to speak of, ye know – just a dram and a joke to pass the time now and then!'

'Aha!' laughed Gourlay, 'there's worse than a drink, by Jove. It puts smeddum in your blood!'

Logan nipped the guard of his arm in heavy playfulness and led him to the Howff.

The House with the Green Shutters

Allan Massie

At the Graham Arms

Allan Massie (*b.* 1938) is one of the most versatile and skilful of the present generation of Scottish novelists. The uncertain sophistication of the dialogue in this scene illustrates Massie's means of conveying the social and psychological tensions of a somewhat decayed modern Scottish county family.

Inevitably the Daimler drew up before the Graham Arms, the journey having been accomplished with no incident, though passengers less blithe might have experienced alarm.

'You had no need for fear,' Colin said, 'I only crash when sober. Motto, therefore, never be sober.'

'Is there much danger of that?' said Kenneth.

'None, for nowadays I only drive when drunk. Ergo, I have eliminated risk. You are about to see Scottish life in its less rosy aspects, though at least there are no vanishing barmen here, and credit is still good. Putatively good.'

They settled themselves at the bar, which was in fact empty except for a drunken labourer having a day off in the corner. Mr Smith's greeting to Colin was tolerant rather than effusive; but tolerance was all Colin sought, even in his present mood. They arranged themselves on stools, Colin and Kenneth flanking Robin and Sally, Colin getting his back to the side wall, between the small window, which was above bar level, and the open fire. It was not lit and a cat slept in the grate. Colin started by holding court. He told them of an expedition to Paris years ago when he had found himself, under the influence of many Pernods, explaining the principles of Existentialism to a shabby old Frenchman.

'He surprised me by having a goodish grip of them, which is something no lecturer ever asks for from his audience, so I pitched it a bit strong, getting more and more abstruse, and was just thinking I was on the point of baffling him, when the waiter came up and said, "*Téléphone, Monsieur Sartre, c'est une jeune fille qui parle...*"'

'I've never drunk Pernod,' said Sally.

'No time like the present for remedying that. Do you have any Pernod, Mr Smith?... alas...alas, *sic transit...*'

He told them of an expedition to the Alps where there had been no snow and they had ended up in Zermatt, drinking the worst white wine in the world – 'Joyce used to like it, which I've always held accounts for Winnegan's Fake' – and 'my friend Giles petulantly kicked a hole in a huge plate glass window and was immediately, but immediately, surrounded by hordes of Switzers all extending their hands, palms uppermost...it's a very comfortable country, Switzerland, despite the white wine, all you've got to do is pay. You can pay for anything, do what damage you like, as long as you've got wads of Swiss francs to shuffle out. Mind you, it's a mysterious country too. Would you believe that in the Gare des Eaux-Vives, which is a little suburban *gare* in Genf, the *specialitiés de la maison* are Nasi-Goreng and Malayan Chicken Curry? Rum.'

He ordered more drinks – 'on that faithful slate, please, Mr Smith. That's where Scotland differs from Switzerreich, there are things you can't buy here.'

'Such as love?' suggested Kenneth.

'Love, my dear, is for sale everywhere.'

He told them of a May Ball in Cambridge which a sometime Financial Secretary to the Treasury had attended in drag – 'a King's man, of course. You're not at King's, are you?' he asked Robin.

He told them of many meetings, comic, bizarre, ridiculous, of trips to Paris, trips to Rome, trips to Naples, trips to Provence, of how London had declined from a leathery imperial city to a sleazy clip-joint, he told them of encounters with gamblers (of a great coup at Monte Carlo), with pimps and politicians, with actresses and gigolos, with Negro boxers and

with a man in a little bar in Rome who had proved painfully to be the judo expert he, Colin, was claiming to be. He told them, he told them, he lost them and in the end didn't so much run down as find a vacancy. He said nothing of death in all this, nor of the corrupting worm. All was jollity, nothing funnier than the odd disaster. 'You mustn't take anything too seriously, baby,' he said. 'My friend Jack once shot a policeman in Athens and lived to smile at the recollection.'

Kenneth said, 'That chap, Morgan, who came in with my my brother and sister-in-law, the one in the safari jacket; don't have anything to do with him. He's a nasty.'

Sally shifted on the bar-stool and crossed her white cottoned legs. She said, 'Look, there's a dartboard. Do you play darts?'

She and Kenneth slipped from the bar-stools.

'Robin,' she said, 'is no good. Keep the score Robin will you.'

'Keep it yourself. I'm having an...'

Sally put the tip of her pink tongue between pink lips as, with deft concentration, she threw her dart. Her neat buttocks pressed themselves against the white seat of her pants, as, on tiptoe, she threw a double twenty.

'Who is this Morgan anyway?' she said. 'He looked rather dishy, I must say.'

Kenneth threw more casually.

'He's a thug,' he said, 'from Rhodesia or some such place. I wouldn't have anything to do with him, if I were you. I think my sister-in-law's a fool.'

'Ooh,' she said and threw a triple twenty.

'Hey, not so fast, you're rather good.'

'There's no point playing games if you're not rather good.'

Kenneth eyed her. 'Quite,' he said, 'you rather bear that out.'

'You must have known a lot of interesting people,' Robin said to Colin.

Colin looked at the two faces reflected in the mirror. 'You would like to meet interesting people,' he said.

'Well, they're better than bores, aren't they?'

'They are bores...'

Their hair grew in the same way, smooth out the lines and it was the same face. Colin could see that, though Robin couldn't. It was easier to read the past than the future.

Why are you living up here now?

Are you afraid of what you will come to?

Colin raised his empty glass and looked at Robin through it; so also the sand ran out of the hourglass.

'Where I made one', he said, 'turn down an empty glass.' He did so. 'Mr Smith, could you oblige...'

The Last Peacock

107

W.S. Graham

The Murdered Drinker

To set the scene. The night
Wind is rushing the moon
Across the winter road.
A mile away a farm
Blinks its oily eye.

Inside snug MacLellan's
Old Rab, the earth's salt,
Knocks one back for the road.
The pub collie lifts
Its nose as he slams the door.

Rab takes the road. The oak
Wood on his left is flying
Away into itself.
At his right hand the big
Branches of elm flail.

By Rhue Corner he stops
And leans on the buzzing pole
And undeservedly
A sick bough of the storm
Falls and murders him.

To set the scene. The night
Wind is rushing the moon
Across the winter road.
A mile away a farm
Blinks its oily eye.

Hugh MacDiarmid

A Drunk Man Looks at the Thistle

This is the opening of the great poem sequence written in 1926 by C.M. Grieve (1892–1978) who wrote under the pen-name of Hugh MacDiarmid.

I amna' fou' sae muckle as tired — deid dune.
It's gey and hard wark' coupin' gless for gless
Wi' Cruivie and Gilsanquhar and the like,
And I'm no' juist as bauld as aince I wes.

The elbuck fankles in the coorse o' time,
The sheckle's no' sae souple, and the thrapple
Grows deef and dour: nae langer up and doun
Gleg as a squirrel speils the Adam's apple.

Forbye, the stuffie's no' the real Mackay.
The sun's sel' aince, as sune as ye began it,
Riz in your vera saul: but what keeks in
Noo is in truth the vilest 'saxpenny planet.'

And as the worth's gane doun the cost has risen.
Yin canna thow the cockles o' yin's hert
Wi'oot ha'en' cauld feet noo, jalousin' what
The wife'll say (I dinna blame her fur't).

It's robbin' Peter to pey Paul at least . . . .
And a' that's Scotch aboot it is the name,
Like a' thing else ca'd Scottish nooadays
—A' destitute o'speerit juist the same.

Robert Chambers

Legal Drinking in the Late Eighteenth Century

Chambers (1802–71), a self-taught scholar of humble origins, was publisher, editor, biographer and antiquary. This piece comes from *Traditions of Edinburgh* (1824), an invaluable collection of anecdotes illustrating the history of the city's social life.

Tavern dissipation, now so rare amongst the respectable classes of the community, formerly prevailed in Edinburgh to an incredible extent, and engrossed the leisure hours of all professional men, scarcely excepting even the most stern and dignified. No rank, class, or profession, indeed, formed an exception to this rule. Nothing was so common in the morning as to meet men of high rank and official dignity reeling home from a close in the High Street, where they had spent the night in drinking. Nor was it unusual to find two or three of his majesty's most honourable Lords of Council and Session mounting the bench in the forenoon in a crapulous state. A gentleman one night stepping into Johnnie Dowie's, opened a side door, and looking into the room, saw a sort of *agger* or heap of snoring lads upon the floor, illumined by the gleams of an expiring candle. 'Wha may thae be, Mr Dowie?' inquired the visitor. 'Oh,' quoth John, in his usual quiet way, 'just twa-three o' Sir Willie's drucken clerks!' – meaning the young gentlemen employed in Sir William Forbes's banking-house, whom, of all earthly mortals, one would have expected to be observers of the decencies...

The *diurnal* of a Scottish judge of the beginning of the last century, which I have perused, presents a striking picture of the habits of men of business in that age. Hardly a night passes without some expense being incurred at taverns, not always of very good fame, where his lordship's associates on the bench were his boon companions in the debauch. One is at a loss to understand how men who drugged their understandings so habitually, could possess any share of vital faculty for the consideration or transaction of business, or how they contrived to make a decent appearance in the hours of duty. But however difficult to be accounted for, there seems no room to doubt that deep drinking was compatible in many instances with good business talents, and even application. Many living men connected with the Court of Session can yet look back to a juvenile period of their lives, when some of the ablest advocates and most esteemed judges were noted for their convivial habits. For example, a famous counsel named Hay, who became a judge under the designation of Lord Newton, was equally remarkable as a Bacchanal and as a lawyer. He considered himself as only the better fitted for business, that he had previously imbibed six bottles of claret; and one of his clerks afterwards declared that the best paper he ever knew his lordship dictate, was done after a debauch where that amount of liquor had fallen to his share. It was of him that the famous story is told of a client calling for him one day at four o'clock, and being surprised to find him at dinner; when, on the client saying to the servant that he had understood five to be Mr Hay's dinner hour, 'Oh but, sir,' said the man, 'it is his *yesterday's dinner!*' M. Simond, who, in 1811, published a *Tour in Scotland*, mentions his surprise on stepping one morning into the Parliament House to find, in the dignified capacity of a judge, and displaying all the gravity suitable to the character, the very gentleman with whom he had spent most of the preceding night in a fierce debauch. This judge was Lord Newton.

Contemporary with this learned lord was another of marvellous powers of drollery, of whom it is told, as a fact too notorious at the time to be concealed, that he was one Sunday morning, not long before church-time, found asleep amongst the paraphernalia of the sweeps, in a shed appropriated to the keeping of these articles, at the end of the Town-Guard-house in the High Street. His lordship, in staggering homeward alone from a tavern during the night, had tumbled into this place, where consciousness did not revisit him till next day. Of another group of clever, but over-convivial lawyers of that age, it is related that, having set to wine and cards on a Saturday evening, they were so cheated out of all sense of time, that the night passed before they thought of separating. Unless they are greatly belied, the people passing along Picardy Place next forenoon, on their way to church, were perplexed by seeing a door open, and three gentlemen issue forth, in all the disorder to be expected after a night of drunken vigils, while a fourth, in his dressing-gown, held the door in one hand and a lighted candle in the other, by way of showing them out!

Traditions of Edinburgh

Will Fyffe

I Belong to Glasgow

The great Scottish comic Will Fyffe (1885–1947) both wrote and sang this famous song. Albert D. Mackie, in his book *The Scottish Comedians* (1973) tells the story (or legend) of its composition:

He was in Central Station in Glasgow and was engaged in conversation with a genial and demonstrative drunk who was laying off about Karl Marx and John Barleycorn with equal enthusiasm. Will asked him: 'Do you belong to Glasgow?' With a broad smile, the drunk replied: 'At the moment, at the moment, Glasgow belongs to me.' Will went home to his digs with the phrase echoing in his head. Like Harry Lauder, who was inspired to write *I Love a Lassie* by a chance remark from a stage-door keeper, and *Roamin' in the Gloamin'* by seeing a couple passing in the twilight on the river bank near Glasgow, Fyffe worked a phrase up to a song which has sometimes been mistakenly regarded as the Scottish National Anthem.

> I belong to Glasgow,
> Dear auld Glasgow toon.
> What's the matter wi' Glasgow
> That it's goin' roon and roon?
> I'm only a common auld working chap,
> As anyone here can see,
> But after a couple of drinks on a Saturday
> Glasgow belongs to me!

David Strachan

Husbands and Wives

The story of which this is an extract is a good example of the
sardonic realism characteristic of many of the younger writers from
Glasgow and the west of Scotland.

Giggling like a couple of schoolgirls, they ran through the snow to their
waiting husbands.

'They have met some French sailors,' Robin was saying. 'Tes seins
sont comme deux colombes.' He fluttered his hands. 'Tes nipples sont
comme des fraises d'Avril. That sort of thing.'

'Quatre colombes,' Harry slurred.

The bar was quiet. People wearing denims were not admitted.

'And now I geeve you a leetle French numbaire,' Robin said, 'about a
Franch sailaire oo come to zee beeg ceety an fall een lov wees leetle
Scoteesh girl.'

'I'll tell you a funny thing,' Harry said. He swirled the whisky round
his glass. 'Elaine's my wife, right? Now I can't imagine Elaine without
clothes. Naked. But I can imagine your Isobel without clothes very
clearly. Isn't that a funny thing?'

'You should see her sister,' Robin said, curving his hands over his
chest. He closed his eyes and shook his head. 'She ees . . . ow you say
. . . exquisite. Married to a Swiss gnome who is . . . ow you say . . . rich.
Money isn't everything, Isobel, I tell her. Money can't buy Appiness.'
He suddenly became tired and serious. 'If the bank doesn't extend their
loan, I'm done for, Harry.' He looked at Harry but Harry was lost in his
own thoughts.

'Damned funny thing that,' Harry said.

'Don't brood,' Robin said. 'When you get drunk, you brood.'

'I love your wife,' Harry said.

'And I love yours.' Robin went over to the bar for two more whiskies.
The barmaid liked him and laughed at whatever he said. Harry watched
them sourly. He envied Robin his easy successes.

'Poor old Isobel,' Robin said when he came back with the whiskies.
'Went to see a new man this morning. A Dr Gibson.'

'Did she always have a bad back?' Harry asked.

'No, not always. I blame her back on Austria. We went there for our
Honeymoon. A pleasant enough place. Salbaach. She had a bad fall. I

think that started it off.' He looked again at his watch. 'I'm worried.'

'Don't worry,' Harry said. 'When you get drunk, you worry'.

'Some Honeymoon! The skiing was good though.'

'Why didn't you go to Paris for your Honeymoon like everyone else?' Harry asked.

'Because the skiing in Paris isn't too good, Harry. That's why we went to Austria.'

Harry fell grumpily silent and Robin whistled irritatingly through his teeth. Harry knew that he bored Robin but then Robin could be pretty boring himself at times. All that French stuff was pretty funny the first time you heard it, but after that it got pretty boring. He knew that they saw a lot of each other because Elaine liked Robin and vice-versa. And he liked Isobel although he wasn't very sure about the vice-versa. Most of the time, he was the odd man out. He knew that. Elaine, Robin and Isobel would get some crazy line of conversation going, funny accents and all, and they would laugh like school-kids, really pleased with how funny they were being and he would be the one who poured the drinks. Their silliness made him feel fuddy-duddy.

Nevertheless he felt his heart lift when Isobel, wearing Elaine's red beret, bright-eyed and laughing, burst into the bar to be followed by Elaine, her black hair flecked with snowflakes. Still laughing, they dropped into the chairs beside Harry and Robin. Robin folded his arms across his chest.

'Me-fella and him-fella wait plenty long time for squaws. Pay plenty glass beads for no-good firewater. Me-fella and him-fella gettum legless.'

'What'll you have?' Harry said, pushing himself to his feet and steadying himself with one hand on the table. 'Isobel?'

'Inebriate of air am I,' Isobel said breathelessly. 'Oh a gin and tonic, thanks, Harry.' Elaine had retrieved her beret and was using it to sweep herself clean of snowflakes.

'Elaine?'

'I'd love a gin and tonic. With lots of ice. Well Robin, what have you been up to of late?'

Harry went to the bar and waited for the barmaid to finish her conversation with a young man at the other end of the bar. While they waited for their drinks to be brought, Robin developed his new line in pidgin banter which kept Elaine amused. Isobel smiled occasionally, letting her eyes wander round the people in the bar, and when she thought no-one was watching, slid her hand down to the small of her back and pressed her fingers against her spine.

Still unserved, Harry turned apologetically from the bar and caught Isobel looking at him. Instinctively he looked away to Robin and Elaine who were still amusing each other, then let his gaze return to Isobel who was still looking at him thoughtfully. Harry returned her gaze with a sheepish smile and a shrug, Isobel gave a slight start, and Harry realized she had been looking at him without seeing him. He coughed to attract the barmaid's attention but she was still leaning across the bar, laughing, talking, listening . . .

Isobel pushed herself upright in the laborious way that pregnant women do, stood tensely for a second or two till her back muscles adjusted to the change in position, then came across to the bar with her right hand held into the small of her back.

'They never serve you if you only stand and wait,' she said. 'They get away with murder. Miss!' she called, loudly and unpleasantly. 'How about doing the job you're paid to do?'

There was an icy silence as the barmaid poured the drinks, polishing each glass with unloving care. Harry found the silence unbearable.

'Your back,' he said as if that had been the subject of previous discussion. 'Would an osteopath perhaps be able to help?' Isobel gave a brief, strangled laugh. Osteopaths! Waitresses! Barmaids! Doctors! Husbands!

'Do you know who was always being asked that?'

Harry glanced nervously at her to see if she really expected a reply to such a question. Her eyes were shut, her face was white, there was a glitter of sweat on her upper lip. 'For . . . God's . . . sake . . . hurry . . . up!' she hissed through closed teeth then with a sharp intake of breath she suddenly opened her eyes wide, and there was Harry looking at her anxiously. 'Atlas!' she said, before he had time to ask what was the matter.

'Three pounds and twenty pence,' the barmaid demanded. Harry fumbled for his wallet.

'Atlas, son of Jupiter.' Again Isobel gave a brief, strangled laugh, put out her right hand so that the fingertips rested on the bar then brought her left hand to her eyes, pressing hard into the sockets with her heel and fingers. Her body weaved slightly and the barmaid, with arms held out to break her fall, leant towards her across the bar.

'Are you all right?' she asked. 'Is she all right?' she asked Harry.

Isobel held her awkward position, seesawing slightly but more from self-induced rocking than from the strain on her one supporting arm.

'Are you all right, Isobel?' Harry asked, glad to see, out of the corner of his eye, Robin hurrying across.

Making small shaking movements of her head, Isobel began to cry, long rasping sobs interspersed with quivering intakes of breath like a hysterical child who has neither self-control nor any apparent regard to the appropriateness of her choice of time and place.

To Elaine, only a few yards away, the event seemed to be taking place in some remote world incredibly distant from herself. She watched the group gather round Isobel then shivered and pulled her coat more tightly around her.

'Areas of Responsibility', in *New Writing, Scotland*, 1983

David Morrison

Brebster Ceilidh

A *ceilidh* (pronounced 'kaily') is a social evening of singing, music-making and story-telling. David Morrison is one of the most prolific and versatile of living Scottish poets and critics. This poem comes from a collection of his and a fellow Scottish poet, Alan Bold's, work entitled *Hammer and Thistle*.

Tam went to the ceilidh
    wanting a lass to lie under him.
Councillor Jones went to the ceilidh
    to show that he had concern
    for the rural community,
    (and to catch votes for the coming local election).
Young Bess, thirsting for romance
    went to the ceilidh
    thinking she might win her knight,
    all white and rosy-cheeked.
Auld Martha went to the ceilidh
    to reassure herself about the sin
    and wayward ways of young ones.
And Sam; why did he go?
    To get drunk on other people's whisky.

All through the evening the dance raged
And the booze flowed as a demon
    catching many a soul for Hell.

In the morning, Tam was wet
    with the lack of a woman.
Councillor Jones awoke with a thick head
    remembering only too well
    that he had annoyed
    those he should not have annoyed.
Young Bess, poor lass, looked in the mirror
    and saw the bruises on her neck;
    she feared the time of month.
Auld Martha resolved to see the Reverend Gunn
    about the sin in his parish.

117

And Sam, what happened to Sam?
  In the morning, Sam, still drinking,
  Thought kindly of the young lass
  who had lain for him;
  He thought of the many
  who had called him fine fellow;
  He laughed as he thought of Auld Martha saying-
    That's guid o ye, Sam,
    Tae see young Bess hame.
    Ye're a fine man, Sam —
    She'll no come tae ony hairm
    In your care.

Sam, drinking other people's whisky
  the morning after the night afore
  knew a Heaven as he crawled on the floor.

Hammer and Thistle

Alexander Stewart

Smugglers' Tricks

'The author of this book', wrote William Watson, Professor of Celtic at the University of Edinburgh in a foreword to the original edition, (1928) from which this extract is taken, 'has probably a fuller knowledge of the traditions of his native parish of Fortingall [near Loch Tay] than any other man now living. His recollections go back to the 'sixties of last century, when Gaelic and all that it implies still flourished among old and young and old habits and customs of life were still, if not practised, at least remembered and spoken of.'

From this time onwards the most frequent charges of law-breaking against the parishioners of Fortingall were smuggling and poaching. But the excise and game laws were regarded by the Highlanders as unjust and tyrannous. The latter especially were a source of ill-feeling against the authorities that imposed them, and frequently also against the officers whose duty it was to enforce them. Breaches of those laws were not regarded as in any sense immoral, and were regularly committed by people who in all other respects were law-abiding citizens of the most irreproachable character. Not only so, but even the magistrates who tried such cases often refused to take a serious view of them. At the beginning of the nineteenth century such offences were tried by the courts of the Justices of the Peace. At Weem, where the local court met, there was often a long list of smuggling and poaching cases before the magistrates; but Francis Mór, the chief of the Macnabs, who usually presided, as a general rule, let the delinquents off lightly.

In such circumstances one can imagine that the task of enforcing these laws was no easy one. Indeed, during the first three quarters of last century, organised and systematic attempts were made to evade these laws, often with an ingenuity worthy of a better cause. No doubt the harshness of the game laws and the poverty of the people were partly responsible for this state of affairs; but law-evasion is always not only a risky but also a demoralising business. As the century proceeded the courts treated breaches of the law less leniently, the game laws themselves were relaxed, and the people came to be as law-abiding in these as in other respects.

Macara in the *Old Statistical Account* relates that towards the end of the eighteenth century smuggling had considerably decreased. In the early part of the nineteenth century it revived again and attained extensive proportions. At that time the duty on spirits had been considerably increased, and during the same period rents were being seriously raised. The small farmers were, therefore, glad to engage in anything that would help them to earn a little money; but it is questionable if many of them ever made much profit out of smuggling. No doubt the element of risk appealed to some of the more daring and adventurous spirits. They probably found the quiet life of a country farmer a somewhat unromantic substitute for the more warlike practices of earlier days. Whatever the cause, illicit stills increased and almost a regular trade in conveying Highland whisky to the southern towns became established. In those days the people stood loyally by each other. If an excise officer appeared in any glen, messengers were sent to the neighbouring hamlets to warn the occupants of the turf and stone bothies that were dug in the sides of the mountain burns for distilling the illicit spirits. The result was that the captures of men or materials were few and far between.

In transporting the products of their labours to market, special precautions had to be taken to prevent discovery. For this purpose women, being less liable to be suspected than men, were often employed. They carried the whisky in tin vessels on their backs. These they covered over with shawls, and, in order to obviate suspicion, they usually carried light baskets with some lace or ribbons in them. On many occasions the

120

carriers travelled by night and wended their way through unfrequented mountain passes. On other occasions spirits were concealed in wool bags or in the bottom of carts, covered over with other goods. In one instance the device was used of carrying the whisky in a cart in which was placed an apparently feeble old man lying on a bed of straw, as if he were in the last stages of illness. On the road to Perth the conveyance was met by a party of excise officers. The latter suspected nothing, and, moved with pity for the old bed-ridden man, asked the driver of the cart what ailed him. To this he replied that he was suffering from the *duibh-leisg*, which they took to be the name of some dreadful malady, but which in reality is the Gaelic phrase for 'back laziness.' On another occasion a large body of excisemen had been sent to intercept any smugglers who might be proceeding towards Crieff or Perth. At the same time a large number of smugglers proceeding southwards with their prohibited wares combined into one band, so that they might be able to overpower the officers of the law should they happen to meet them. The two bodies met at Corriemuckloch, near the entrance to the Small Glen, and the result was a conflict in which several men were injured.

The smugglers not only contrived ingeniously to keep themselves and their stills and other distilling utensils out of the hands of the excise officers, but some of them even made daring attempts to recover their utensils after they had been seized by the excisemen. Donald C——, one of the boldest of smugglers, had his bothy at the side of a burn behind Schiechallion. It was discovered by the excisemen, and they removed his whole distilling plant to the little inn in Foss, where they decided to put up for the night. In order that the booty might be perfectly secure, it was deposited in the bedroom where they themselves were sleeping. Then with locked doors and, as they supposed, well secured against any would-be intruder, they slept soundly, oblivious of danger. But Donald was determined that they should not get away with his gear. They occupied an upper room, but it had an end or gable window. To this window Donald, in the dead of night, made his way with the aid of some planks. He quickly unfastened it, entered the room, threw the excisemen's shoes through the window, and with a jingling noise made off with his precious wares. The gaugers, as the excisemen were usually called, though wakened by the noise, spent some little time searching for their shoes, so that Donald was some distance ahead of them. The search for their shoes proving vain, they gave pursuit in their stockings' soles, but Donald proved too fleet for them. Before his pursuers could make up on him, he was able to reach a peat hollow, where he hid his gear, and the excise officers were never able to find it. When he took them out of this hiding place, he sold them to another man and forsook the illicit trade once for all.

A Highland Parish, or the History of Fortingall

Anonymous

Drap of Capie ...O

David Herd (1731−1810), from whose compilation of 1776 this song comes, was the greatest collector in the eighteenth century of old Scottish songs and ballads and his anthology provided an invaluable quarry for later collectors, editors and song-writers, Burns among them.

There liv'd a wife in our gate-end,
    She lo'ed a drap of capie ...O,
And all the gear that e'er she gat,
    She slipt it in her gabie ...O.

Upon a frosty winter's night,
    The wife had got a drapie ...O;
And she had pish'd her coats sae weil,
    She could not find the patie ...O.

But she's awa' to her goodman,
    They ca'd him TAMIE LAMIE ...O.
Gae ben and fetch the cave to me,
    That I may get a dramie ...O.

TAMIE was an honest man,
    Himself he took a drapie ...O,
It was nae weil out o'er his craig,
    Till she was on his tapie ...O.

She paid him weil, baith back and side,
    And fair she creish'd his backie ...O,
And made his skin baith blue and back,
    And gar'd his shoulders crackie ...O.

Then he's awa' to the malt barn,
    And he has ta'en a pockie ...O,
He put her in, baith head and tail,
    And cast her o'er his backie ...O.

The carling spurn'd wi' head and feet,
  The carle he was sae ackie . . . O,
To ilka wall that he came by,
  He gar'd her head play knackie . . . O.

Goodman, I think you'll murder me,
  My brains you out will knockie . . . O,
He gi'd her ay the other hitch,
  Lie still, you devil's buckie . . . O.

Goodman, I'm like to make my burn,
  O let me out, good TAMIE . . . O;
Then he set her upon a stane,
  And bade her pish a damie . . . O.

Then TAMIE took her aff the stane,
  And put her in the pockie . . . O,
And when she did begin to spurn,
  He lent her ay a knockie . . . O.

Away he went to the mill-dam,
  And there ga'e her a duckie . . . O,
And ilka chiel that had a stick,
  Play'd thump upon her backie . . . O.

And when he took her hame again,
  He did hing up the pockie . . . O,
At her bed-side, as I hear say,
  Upon a little knagie . . . O.

And ilka day that she up-rose,
  In naithing but her smockie . . . O,
Sae soon as she look'd o'er the bed,
  She might behold the pockie . . . O.

Now all ye men, baith far and near,
  That have a drunken tutie . . . O,
Duck you your wives in time of year,
  And I'll lend you the pockie . . . O,

The wife did live for nineteen years,
  And was fu' frank and cuthie . . . O,
And ever since she got the duck,
  She never had the drouthie . . . O.

At last the carling chanc'd to die,
    And TAMIE did her bury . . . O,
And for the publick benefit,
    He has gar'd print the curie . . . O.

And this he did her motto make;
    Here lies an honest luckie . . . O,
Who never left the drinking trade,
    Until she got a duckie . . . O.

Ancient and Modern Scottish Songs

William McIlvanney

Kathleen's Wedding Party

This is from William McIlvanney's (*b*. 1936) great novel of working class life in an industrial town in the west of Scotland in the first part of this century.

Mairtin stood translating everything into himself. The glass in his hand took wilful reflections from everything around him. The bulge of his belly was satisfaction. One foot danced in stasis, his family moving threaded on his thoughts. In the moustache years were held in arrested avalanche.

Each dance was a relationship. The steps created a convention within which they could celebrate themselves, uncles, cousins, aunts, neighbours, friends, advancing, receding, intersecting, pivoting on one another, all conforming to patterns whose law was whimsy. The music quickened the whole thing into compulsion.

In the flare of sudden movement, round the corner of a comment, faces bobbed, piked on exertion, a group sat in an alcove of private conversation. Privacies became public.

A fat man's galluses burst. He had taken off his jacket and waistcoat to be comfortable. One strand of the braces twanged over his shoulder like a fractured harp-string. One side of his trousers drooped, revealing the tops of home-made drawers of scarlet wool. Tadger Daly stood bowed in the middle of the floor, lockjawed with laughter.

Jenny's Uncle James revealed the secret of how to put water and whisky in the same glass and keep them separate. While the younger children played at sliding along the edge of the dance-floor, Angus, hiding at the end of a corridor, showed Conn how to smoke, and drank an inch of stale beer from a tumbler which had been left below a chair. The Co-operative Hall was a masque of faces lurid with enjoyment, luminous with sweat. Even Jenny's mother, in the presence of so much drink, kept a festive smile clenched like a fading rose between her teeth.

The dress, an heirloom starched and laundered specially for Kathleen, shed radiance wherever she went. At half past seven in the morning, she had stood in the living-room, imprisoned in its stiff whiteness, waiting for the cab to take her to chapel. Her strange presence muted the rest of the room, made it seem drab, a cocoon that had belied its contents. Her father and brothers were almost shy, embarrassed by what they hadn't seen before. Her mother fussed gently, possessing for the last time. Kathleen asked plaintive irrelevant questions about her appearance, innocent of her own transformation. It wasn't beauty, or anything that could be objectively named. It was simply Kathleen, the blackness of her hair blued subtly by the whiteness of the veil, her eyes deepened into an awareness of what she thought the day meant to her, her body's ripeness, her oval face achieving the brief perfection of itself.

Conn's Uncle Sammy dropped a glass. Having been accused of being drunk, he offered to stand on his hands to prove sobriety. To have his hands free for demonstration, he put his glass down on a chair that had been taken away minutes ago. It was the beer he didn't take that finally couped him. Seeing the exploded shards of glass, he dismissed any suggestion of a brush and shovel.

'Nae man that wisny sober could pick up a' these bits withoot an injury. Right?'

His wife escorted him home five minutes later, handcuffed with a bloodstained dish-towel.

Old Conn enjoyed himself with his pipe and a little beer. All evening people arrived at his chair to talk, laugh, and go away. He smiled much. Reflected in his gentle eyes, the dancers whirled and flung across a desert.

Jack said, 'Ah never expected tae enjoy ma ain waddin' as much. An' the best o' it's tae come.'

He tried to make sure he spoke to as many people as possible. He moved among a minefield of suspicions and survived. Older women watched, waited for him, listened, nodded.

'He seems a nice boay.'

'A guid wey wi' him.'

'Aye. At least they're beginnin' weel enough.'

The children gave way first, so that the evening died slowly and piecemeal among them. One lay asleep on a window-ledge, cushioned on a jacket. Another slept across two chairs, another on his mother's knee. Two small brothers niggled each other half-heartedly, wrangling with their tiredness. The songs grew sadder. 'The Nameless Lassie' was strangled at leisure. Only a few couples still soft-shoed around the floor, as if caught up in a habit they couldn't break. A woman sat staring across the bleakness of tomorrow. The empty glasses covered two trestle-tables. Three men, caged in their own agreement, picked fleas from one another's egos. The band were taking longer between tunes. The dark silence of the town outside was seeping into the place like gas, deadening them.

It was a bright moon, the cadaver of daylight. The unusualness of being abroad together in the early hours of the morning heightened their awareness of one another. They were more a family for being alone in the lunar emptiness of the town. Angus walked slightly ahead of Jenny, whose hand was on Conn's shoulder. Mick and Tam came behind them, talking. Tam, proud of the social ease and straightforward likeableness he had seen in Mick this evening, was pleased to let him do most of the talking, while Tam himself silently memorised his happiness so that he could keep it with him after tonight. Kathleen, he thought, was well married. Jack should make a good man. Everything had been fine − the meal, the drink, the dancing. They couldn't really afford it, except that you had to be able to afford what your children deserved. There wasn't any other way to live.

Docherty

Anonymous

The Tarves Rant

This lively, modern Aberdeenshire ballad, is included in the collection of folk songs compiled by Gavin Greig, and edited by Kenneth Goldstein and Arthur Argo.

Come all ye jolly hireman lads,
  And listen unto me;
I'll tell to you a story,
  Without a word o' lee.

My name I needna mention,
  It's hardly worth the while,
I am a jolly bailie lad,
  Near Tarves I do dwell.

I canna work your horses,
  I canna haud your ploo,
Nor cut nor build in harvest,
  But I can feed a coo.

It happened on an evening
  To Tarves we did go,
To get a dram and hae some fun, —
  The truth I'll let you know.

When we arrived at Tarves,
  To D——'s we did pad,
And there we got some music,
  That made our hearts right glad.

That man that played the music,
  His name I needna hide,
He was a jolly ploughman lad,
  They ca'd him Ironside.

Some was there for boots and shoes,
  And some was there for clothes;
But he was there for treacle,
  He being on his brose.

Few was there that I did know,
  And as few there knew me;
But there was one among the rest
  That tried to bully me.

It's then to P——'s we did go,
  To try and get some fun;
There I was sore ensnared
  Wi' the maiden o' the inn.

She was a lovely maiden,
  The maiden that she be —
Two rosy cheeks, twa rollin' e'en,
  And a lovely girl was she.

We sat and drank, and merry were,
  We drank — I think na shame;
When eleven o'clock began to strike,
  We steered our course for hame.

It was there I lost my comrade,
  And on him I did cry;
Just at that very moment
  A man in blue came by.

He told me very plainly,
  If I didna hold my tongue,
He would take me into custody
  Before that it was long.

He took me roughly by the arm,
  And dragged me to the inn;
'T was there we fought in earnest,
  For it didna end in fun.

He tried to haul me through the door,
  His strength he didna spare,
But I did plainly show to him
  That it would need a pair.

But surely I'm a profligant,
  A villain to the bone,
To tear the coat from off his back,
  It being not his own.

But soon assistance came to him,
  They dragged me through the door,
There I was made a prisoner,
  And left to think it o'er.

A sudden thought came in my mind, —
  I up the window drew;
Twa willing hands did pull me out,
  That didna like the blue.

I think the folks in Tarves
  A jail wad need to get,
For to lock up their prisoners,
  And nae let them escape.

For surely it main be a sin
  To break the Sabbath day,
Searching for their prisoners
  When they do run away.

I've something more to tell you,
  But not to my disgrace;
To Aberdeen I was brought up,
  Just for to plead my case.

When I received my sentence,
  I heard it like a shot;
There was thirty shillings for a fine
  And fifteen for the coat.

Now all ye jolly hireman lads,
  A warning take by me,
When you go down to Tarves,
  And nae get on the spree.

Just go and get your eerant,
  And steer your course for hame,
And when a row it does begin,
  Ye winna get the blame.

Folk Songs of the North East

Hugh Foulis

Confidence

Hugh Foulis was the men name adopted by Neil Munro (1864–
1930) for his more light-hearted works of fiction, including the
popular stories of Para Handy (Peter, son of Sandy), skipper of the
west coast 'puffer'.

The Captain of the *Vital Spark* and his mate were solemnly drinking
beer in a Greenock public-house, clad in their best shore-going togs, for
it was Saturday. Another customer came in — a bluff, high-coloured,
English-spoken individual with an enormous watch-chain made of what
appeared to be mainly golden nuggets in their natural state, and a ring
with a diamond bulging out so far in it that he could hardly get his hand
into his trousers pocket. He produced a wad of bank-notes, peeled one
off, put it down on the counter with a slap, and demanded gin and
ginger.

'A perfect chentleman!' said Para Handy to his mate in a whisper; 'you
can aalways tell them! He'll likely have a business somewhere.'

The opulent gentleman took his glass of gin and ginger to a table and
sat down, lit a cigar, and proceeded to make notes in a pocket-book.

'That's the worst of wealth,' said Dougie philosophically; 'you have to
be aalways tottin' it up in case you forget you have it. Would you care
for chust another, Peter? I think I have a shullin'.'

Another customer came in — apparently a seaman, with a badge of a
well-known shipping line on his cap.

'Hello, bully boys!' he said heartily. 'Gather around; there's a letter
from home! What are we going to have? In with your pannikins, lively
now, and give it a name,' and he ordered glasses round, excluding the
auriferous gentleman who was taking notes behind.

'Looks like a bloomin' Duke!' he remarked in an undertone to Para
Handy. 'One of them ship-owners, likely; cracker-hash and dandy-funk
for Jack and chicken and champagne wine for Mister Bloomin' Owner!
Ours is a dog's life, sonnies, but I don't care now, I'm home from
Callao!'

'Had you a good trup?' asked Para Handy, with polite anxiety.

'Rotten!' said the seaman tersely. 'What's your line? Longshore, eh?'
and he scrutinised the crew of the *Vital Spark*.

'Chust that!' said Para Handy mildly. 'Perusin' aboot the Clyde wi' coals and doin' the best we can.'

'Then I hope the hooker's your own, my boy, for there's not much bloomin' money in it otherwise,' said the seaman; and Para Handy, not for the first time, fell a victim to his vanity.

'Exactly' he said, with a pressure on the toe of Dougie's boot; 'I'm captain and owner too; the smertest boat in the tred,' and he jingled a little change he had in his pocket.

'My name's Tom Wilson,' volunteered the seaman. 'First mate of the *Wallaby*, with an extra master's papers, d——n your eyes! And I've got five-and-twenty bloomin' quids in my pocket this very moment; look at that!' He flourished a wad of notes that was almost as substantial as the one displayed a little before by the gentleman with the nugget watch-chain.

'It's a handy thing to have aboot ye,' said Para Handy sagely, jingling his coppers eloquently. 'But I aalways believe in gold mysel'; you're not so ready to lose it.'

'I've noticed that mysel',' said Dougie solemnly.

Tom Wilson ordered another round, and produced a watch which he confidently assured them was the finest watch of its kind that money could buy. It had an alarm bell, and luminous paint on the hands and dial permitted you to see the time on the darkest night without a light.

'Well, well! issn't that cluvver!' exclaimed Para Handy. 'They'll be makin' them next to boil a cup o' tea. It would cost a lot o' money? I'm no' askin', mind you; I wass chust remarkin'.'

'Look here!' cried Tom Wilson impulsively; 'I'll give the bloomin' clock to the very first man who can guess what I paid for it.'

'Excuse me, gentlemen,' said the man with the nugget watch-chain, putting away his note-book and pencil. 'I'd like to see that watch,' and they joined him at the table, where he generously ordered another round. He gravely examined the watch, and guessed that it cost about twenty pounds.

'Yes, but you must mention the exact figure,' said its owner.

'Well, I guess two-and-twenty sovereigns,' said the other, and Tom Wilson hastily proceeded to divest himself of the chain to which it had been originally attached. 'It's yours!' he said; 'you've guessed it, and you may as well have the bloomin' chain as well. That's the sort of sunny boy I am!' and he beamed upon the company with the warmth of one whose chief delight in life was to go round distributing costly watches.

'Waas I not chust goin' to say twenty-two pounds!' said Para Handy with some chagrin.

'I knew it wass aboot that,' said Dougie; 'chenuine gold!'

The lucky winner of the watch laughed, put it into his pocket, and took out the wad of notes, from which he carefully counted out twenty-two pounds, which he thrust upon Tom Wilson.

'There you are!' he said; 'I wouldn't take your watch for nothing, and it happens to be the very kind of watch I've been looking for.'

'But you have only got my word for it, Mister, that it's worth that money,' protested Mr Wilson.

The stranger smiled. 'My name's Denovan,' he remarked; 'I'm up here from Woolwich on behalf of the Admiralty to arrange for housin' the torpedo workers in first-rate cottage homes with small back gardens. What does the Lords o' the Admiralty say to me? The Lords o' the Admiralty says to me, "Mr Denovan, you go and fix up them cottage homes, and treat the people of Greenock with confidence." I'm a judge of men, I am, bein' what I am, and the principle I go on is to trust my fellow-men. If you say two-and-twenty pounds is the value of this watch, I say two-and-twenty pounds is the value of this watch, I say two-and-twenty it is, and there's an end of it!'

Mr Wilson reluctantly put the notes in his pocket, with an expression of the highest admiration for Mr Denovan's principles, and Para Handy experienced the moral stimulation of being in an atmosphere of exceptional integrity and unlimited wealth. 'Any wan could see you were the perfect chentleman,' he confessed to Mr Denovan, ducking his head at him. 'What way are they aal keepin' in Woolwich?'

'I took you for a bloomin' ship-owner at first,' said Mr Wilson. 'I didn't think you had anything to do with the Admiralty.'

'I'm its right-hand man,' replied Mr Denovan modestly. 'If you're thinkin' of a nice cottage home round here with front plot and small back garden, I can put you in, as a friend, for one at less than half what anybody else would pay.'

'I haven't any use for a bloomin' house unless there was a licence to it,' said Mr Wilson cheerfully.

Mr Denovan looked at him critically. 'I like the look of you,' he remarked impressively. 'I'm a judge of men, and just to back my own opinion of you, I'll put you down right off for the first of the Admiralty houses. You needn't take it; you could sell it at a profit of a hundred pounds tomorrow; I don't ask you to give me a single penny till you have made your profit,' and Mr Denovan, producing his pocket-book, made a careful note of the transaction lest he might forget it. ' "Treat the people of Greenock with confidence," says the Lords of the Admiralty to me; now, just to show my confidence in you, I'll hand you back your watch, and my own watch, and you can go away with them for twenty minutes.'

'All right, then; just for a bloomin' lark,' agreed Tom Wilson, and with both watches and the colossal nugget-chain, he disappeared out of the public-house.

'That's a fine, smart, honest-lookin', manly fellow!' remarked Mr Denovan admiringly.

'Do you think he'll come back wi' the watches?' said Dougie dubiously.

'Of course he will,' replied Mr Denovan. 'Trust men, and they'll trust you. I'll lay you a dollar he would come back if he had twenty watches and all my money as well.'

This opinion was justified. Mr Wilson returned in less than five minutes, and restored the watches to their owner.

'Well, I'm jeegered!' said Para Handy, and ordered another round out of admiration for such astounding honesty.

'Would you trust me?' Mr Denovan now asked Tom Wilson.

'I would,' said the seaman heartily. 'Look here; I've five-and-twenty bloomin' quid, and I'll let you go out and walk the length of the railway station with them.'

'Done!' said Mr Denovan, and possessed of Wilson's roll of notes, went out of the public-house.

'Peter,' said Dougie to the Captain, 'do you no' think one of us should go efter him chust in case there's a train for Gleska at the railway station?'

But Tom Wilson assured them he had the utmost confidence in Mr Denovan, who was plainly a tip-top gentleman of unlimited financial resources, and his confidence was justified, for Mr Denovan not only returned with the money, but insisted on adding a couple of pounds to it as a recognition of Mr Wilson's sporting spirit.

'I suppose you Scotch chaps don't have any confidence? said Mr Denovan to the Captain.

'Any amount!' said Para Handy.

'Well, just to prove it,' said Mr Denovan, 'would you be willin' to let our friend Wilson here, or me, go out with the five-pound note of yours?'

'I havena the five pounds here, but I have it in the boat,' said the Captain. 'If Dougie 'll wait here, I'll go down for it. Stop you, Dougie, with the chentlemen.'

Some hours later Dougie turned up on the *Vital Spark* to find the Captain in his bunk, and sound asleep.

'I thocht you were comin' wi' a five-pound note?' he remarked on wakening him. 'The chentlemen waited, and better waited, yonder on you, and they werena pleased at aal. They said you surely hadna confidence.'

'Dougie,' said the Captain, 'I have the greatest confidence, but I have the five pounds, too. And if you had any money in your pocket it's no' with Mr Denovan I would leave you.'

Para Handy and Other Tales

James Kennaway

Officers' Mess in a Highland Barracks

This extract is from Kennaway's first novel, published in 1956, about conflicts within a Highland regiment. Kennaway (*b.* 1928) was killed in a car accident in 1968.

There is a high wall that surrounds Campbell Barracks, and in the winter there is often a layer of crusted snow on top of it. No civilian rightly knows what happens behind that grey wall but everybody is always curious, and people were more than ever curious one January a year or two ago.

The north wind had blown most of the snow to the side of the barrack square, and not a soul walked there; not a canteen cat. In the guardroom the corporal commanding the picket was warming his fingers on a mug of hot tea, and the metalwork on the sentry's rifle was sticky with frost. In the bathhouse the Battalion plumber was using a blow-lamp on the pipes, and he had reached the stage of swearing with enjoyment. The sergeants were in their Mess, singing to keep themselves warm, and drinking to keep themselves singing. National Servicemen wished they were home in their villas, and horn-nailed Regulars talked of Suez; even the bandboys wished they were back at borstal. In the Married Quarters, the Regimental Sergeant-Major, Mr Riddick, was sandwiched between his fire and his television set.

But it was warm in the Officers' Mess. Dinner was over, and the Queen had had her due. The long dining-room with the low ceiling was thick with tobacco smoke. The regimental silver cups, bowls and goblets shone in the blaze of the lights above the table, and from the shadows past colonels, portrayed in black and white, looked down at the table with glassy eyes. Two pipers, splendid in their scarlet, marched round and round the table playing the tunes of glory. The noise of the music was deafening, but on a dinner night this was to be expected.

The officers who owned 'Number Ones' were in their blue tunics and tartan trews. Sitting back from the table they crossed their legs and admired their thighs and calves. They moved their feet and felt the comfort of the leather Wellingtons that fitted closely to the ankle. Only one or two of the subalterns who could not rise to Number Ones were wearing khaki tunics and kilts. But, drunk to the stage of excited physical consciousness, they too crossed their legs and glanced with anxious pride at their knees. They had folded their stockings to make the most of the muscles of their legs, and they wore nothing under their kilts. Some were anxious that the dinner should finish early giving them time to visit their women. Others of a more philosophic turn of mind had resigned themselves by now. They had ruled out the idea of visiting a woman and they were now falling into a slow stupor. Both sets of officers would in the end return to their bunks, thoroughly dispirited, and breathless with the cold of three o'clock in the morning. The lover as likely as not, if he were still a subaltern, would be disappointed to the point of pain, and the philosopher, bowing patiently and bowing low to the inevitable, would be sick. And both would live to fight another day.

But it was at this point in the evening, when the pipers played, that the officers could see most clearly how the night would end. Their fate lay in the hands of the man sitting half way up the table, and in spite of the Mess President at the head, nobody could deny that the table was commanded by the unforgettable figure of Acting Lieutenant-Colonel Jock Sinclair, D.S.O. (and bar).

The Colonel's face was big and smooth and red and thick. He had blue eyes — they were a little bloodshot now — and his voice was a sergeant's. His hair, which was thin, was brushed straight back with brilliantine. It was not a bit grey. The Colonel did not look broad because he was also deep, and had the buttons on his tunic been fastened there would have been little creases running across his chest and stomach. But at times such as this he was inclined to unfasten his buttons. He had even unfastened the top two buttons of his trews this evening and his striped shirt protruded through the gap in the tartan. His trews were skin tight and it looked as if he need only brace his muscles to tear the seams apart. In his lap he nursed a very large tumbler of whisky, and he tapped his foot on the ground as the pipers played. He did not seem to find the music too loud.

From time to time he glanced round the table, and other officers when they caught his eye quickly turned away while he continued to stare. The look in his eye was as flat as the sole of his polished boot.

He had already made the pipers play three extra tunes that night, and as they played *The Green Hills* for the second time he hummed, and the music comforted him. He put his glass on the table when the room was silent again.

'Get away with you,' he said, surprisingly kindly, to the Corporal-Piper and as the pipers marched out of the room the officers applauded in their usual way: they banged their fists on the table and stamped their feet on the floor-boards. Jock sent orders that the pipers should be given double whiskies, then he leant back in his chair and groaned, while his officers talked. It was some minutes later when one of the younger

137

subalterns at the far end of the table caught his attention. Jock tipped forward in his seat and put his clenched fists on the table. The flat eye grew narrow; the meat on his face quivered, and along the table conversation died on the lips. He made a suppressed sound which was still something of a shout:

'MacKinnon, boy!' Then he lowered his voice to a hiss. 'For Christ's sake smoke your cigarette like a man. Stop puffing at it like a bloody debutante.' He moved his hand as though he were chucking away a pebble, and he spoke loudly again. 'Get on with you; smoke, laddie, smoke . . .'

There was silence in the room as the young subaltern put his cigarette to his lips. He held it rather stiffly between two fingers and he half closed his eyes as he drew in the tobacco smoke. There was still a hush. He looked nervously at his Colonel as he took the cigarette from his lips. Even the movement of his wrist as he brought the cigarette down to the plate had something inescapably feminine about it, and this made Jock shake his fist. The boy's mouth was now full of smoke and he sat very still, with his eyes wide open.

'Go on then, laddie; draw it in, draw it in.'

MacKinnon took a deep breath which made him feel a little dizzy and he was glad that the Colonel could not resist a joke at this point. The sound of his little cough was drowned by the laughter that greeted his Colonel's witticism. Jock looked from side to side.

'We've got laddies that've never put it in, I know,' he said with both a wink and a nod. 'What I didn't know is how we've one who can't even draw it in, eh?' When he laughed the veins on his temple stood out. Then the laugh, as usual, deteriorated into a thick cough, and he shook backwards and forwards in an attempt to control it.

The officers were a mixed collection. One or two of them, such as Major Macmillan, who was perpetually sunburnt, seemed very much gentlemen, although they too laughed at Jock's jokes. The others, if not gentlemen, were Scotsmen. The younger they were the larger were their jaws, the older they were the fatter were their necks, except of course for the Quartermaster, Dusty Millar, who had no neck at all.

At last Jock recovered himself. 'Aye,' he said, with a final cough, 'aye . . . Well gentlemen, I have news for you.'

Someone at the far end of the table was still talking.

'All of you, you ignorant men.' Jock raised his voice. 'News that'll affect you all.' He paused. 'Tomorrow there's a new colonel coming, and he'll be taking over the Battalion. D'you hear? D'you hear me now?'

All the officers hesitated. Their jaws dropped and they leant forward to look at Jock, who was looking at his tumbler.

Macmillan had a light-comedy voice. He touched his fair hair with his hand and he said, 'Come, Jock, you're pulling our legs.'

'Aye,' someone said uncertainly, disbelievingly. 'That's it, isn't it?'

'What I'm telling you is true.' Jock took a sip of his drink. 'Ask Jimmy Cairns. Jimmy knows right enough.'

Cairns, who was his Adjutant, did not know what to say but felt it was a time when something should be said. He moved his hands, and he frowned,

'That's the way of it,' he said.

'Och . . .' The Quartermaster moaned, and others echoed him.

'That's not right,' one said; and another, 'It can't be true.' The Battalion without Jock as C.O. seemed then an impossibility.

Jock raised his hand in the smoky air.

'We didn't ask for comments,' he said. Then, glancing at the younger officers at the far end of the table, some of whom did not seem so dismayed by the news, he added, 'One way or the other,' and he showed his teeth when he grinned. He grew solemn again and drew his hand down his face and wagged his head, as if to clear his vision. 'It's just a fact,' he said slowly, 'it's just a fact,' and he leant back in his chair again.

Major Charlie Scott, who sat next to Jock, had an after-dinner habit of stroking his large red moustache, but he dropped his hand to ask, 'What's his name, eh?'

'Basil Barrow.'

'Major Barrow?' a clear-voiced subaltern said at once. 'He lectured at Sandhurst. He's an expert on Special . . .' Suddenly aware that he had sounded a little too enthusiastic, his voice trailed away. He looked around, brushed some ash from his trews, and continued in a nonchalant tone, 'Oh, he's really quite all right; they say he's frightfully bright upstairs.' The officers looked towards the Colonel again. They were gradually recovering.

'Aye,' Jock said. 'He went to Oxford, if that means anything. They say he was a great success as a lecturer or whatever he was. Quite a turn with the cadets.' He gave a malicious grin and another big wink. Then he belched and made a sour face. He took another drink of whisky.

'Colonel Barrow's a man about forty-four. Eton — aye, it's right, what I'm telling you — Eton and Oxford. He joined the Regiment in 1935 and he was only with it a year or two before being posted on special duties. He has some languages, so it seems. It's as young Simpson says. He's bright upstairs. He got the M.C. and he was taken prisoner pretty early on.' Jock swung his eyes around the table. 'I know all about him; you see that?'

'There was a fellow we used to call Barrow Boy. D'you remember him? A lightweight chap; good at fencing, if I recall.'

'I remember. Good Lord, yes.'

Jock spoke again. 'That's the same chum. That's him. He was well placed in the Pentathlon sometime just before the war.' He grew suddenly tired of the subject. 'Well, he's to command the Battalion and I'll have another tumbler of whisky.'

A Mess steward dashed forward and replaced the empty glass with a full one. On nights like this Jock's drinks were lined up on a shelf just inside the pantry door; lined up in close formation.

'And what about you, Jock?' Cairns asked.

'Aye. And what about me, china?'

'You staying on?'

'Unless you're going to get rid of me, Jimmy.'

Cairns knew just how far he could go with Jock.

'I thought there might be a chance of it.'

Jock was about to smile when the same subaltern who had known Barrow interrupted. 'Staying on as second-in-command, you mean?' and he was too young and a little too well spoken to get away with it. His seniors glanced immediately at the Colonel. Jock eyed the boy with real hatred, and there was a very long pause.

One of the stewards by the pantry door all but dropped his salver; his eyes grew wide, and he felt the hair rising at the back of his neck. Goblets and glasses poised in the air, whisky stayed in the mouth, unswallowed, and the swirly cloud of smoke above Jock's head for one instant seemed perfectly still.

Jock spoke very sourly, and quietly. 'So may it please you, Mr Simpson,' was what he said, looking back to his tumbler.

'Oh, I'm glad you're not leaving us, sir.' But the answer came too glibly. Jock shrugged and gave a little snigger. He spoke as if he did not care whether he was heard. 'You're away off net, laddie . . . and, Mr Simpson?'

It was fairly easy to see that Mr Simpson had been a prefect at school. He looked the Colonel straight in the eye and he never quite closed his mouth.

'Yes, sir?'

'No "Sirs" in the Mess. Christian names in the Mess except for me and I'm "Colonel". I call you just what I feel like. O.K.?'

'Yes, Colonel.'

'Yes, Colonel . . . Now, gentlemen; now then. This is Jock's last supper and there'll be a round of drinks on me. Even one for Mr Simpson. Corporal!'

'Sir.'

'Whisky. For the gentlemen that like it and for the gentlemen who don't like it, whisky.'

He turned apologetically to Charlie Scott, who was still stroking his moustache.

'I'm no good at talking at the best of times, Charlie, and tonight I'm no coping at all. Will we have the pipers back? It fills in the gaps.'

'Whatever you say, Jock; it's your night.'

'Aye.' Jock opened his eyes very wide: this was one of his mannerisms. 'Aye,' he used to say, then with his eyes wide open he would add a little affirmative noise. It was an open-mouthed 'mm'. Aye, and a-huh. 'Well I say we'll have the pipers.' He leant back in his chair and addressed one of the stewards who was hurrying by with a bottle. 'Laddie, call the pipers.'

'This minute, sir.'

'Just "Sir".' He made a gesture with his flat hand: a little steadying gesture. It was the same gesture that had steadied men in the desert, in Italy, France, Germany and Palestine. 'Just "Sir". That's all you need say.' Then he sighed, and he said, 'Aye, Charlie.' He dug the point of his knife into the table-cloth again and again as he talked. He first made a hole with the knife and gradually he widened it.

'. . . And you'll have a tune, and I'll have a tune, and Macmillan here'll have a tune, and I'll have another tune. Charlie, why the hell d'you grow that moustache so big?'

Major Charlie Scott continued to stroke it with his fingers. His great green eyes grew wide, under the shepherd's eyebrows. He could think of no explanation.

'Dunno; I'm sure. Just grew.'

Jock leant his chair back on two legs again and his arms fell down by his sides. 'And you're not the great talker yourself.'

''Fraid not.'

'No . . . Well, let's have the music. *Ho-ro, my Nut Brown Maiden* for me, and for you, Charlie?'

'*The Cock o' the North*.' Jock tipped forward at that. The legs of the chair creaked as they pitched on the floor again.

'Yon's the Gordons' tune!'

'I still like it.'

Jock screwed up his face: he was genuinely worried.

'But yon's a cheesy tune, Charlie.'

Charlie Scott shrugged.

Jock leant forward to persuade him. 'Laddie, I was with them for a wee while. They didn't like me, you know; no. And Jock didn't care much for them, neither.'

'Really?'

'Can you no think of a better tune?'

'Myself, I like *The Cock o' the North*.' Charlie Scott put another cigarette in his holder.

Jock laughed and the veins stood out again. He slapped his thigh and that made a big noise.

'And I love you, Charlie; you're a lovely man. You're no a great talker, right enough. But you've a mind of your own . . . Aye, pipers, and where have you been?'

'Pantry, sir.'

'Are you sober?'

'Sir.'

'You'd bloody well better be, and that's a fact. You're no here to get sick drunk the same as the rest of us are.'

The drones began as the bladders filled with air. The pipers marched round and round again. The room grew smokier, and the officers sat close into their chairs as the drink began to flow. The stewards never rested.

Tunes of Glory

Martin Martin

Ceremonial Drinking in the Western Isles

Published in 1703, this extract comes from the pioneer descriptive work which Dr Johnson read before undertaking his tour of the Hebrides with Boswell. It was written by the factor of the laird of MacLeod.

The manner of drinking used by the chief men of the isles is called in their language Streah, *i.e.*, a round; for the company sat in a circle, the cup-bearer filled the drink round to them, and all was drunk out whatever the liquor was, whether strong or weak; they continued drinking sometimes twenty-four, sometimes forty-eight hours. It was reckoned a piece of manhood to drink until they became drunk, and there were two men with a barrow attending punctually on such occasions. They stood at the door until some became drunk, and they carried them upon the barrow to bed, and returned again to their post as long as any continued fresh, and so carried off the whole company one by one as they became drunk. Several of my acquaintance have been witnesses to this custom of drinking, but it is now abolished.

Among persons of distinction it was reckoned an affront put upon any company to broach a piece of wine, ale, or aquavitae and not to see it all drunk out at one meeting. If any man chance to go out from the company, though but for a few minutes, he is obliged upon his return, and before he take his seat, to make an apology for his absence in rhyme; which, if he cannot perform, he is liable to such a share of the reckoning as the company think fit to impose; which custom obtains in many places still, and is called *beanchiy bard*, which in their language signifies the poet's congratulating the company.

A Description of the Western Islands of Scotland

Peter F. Anson

Fisherfolk Customs

Peter Anson lived for many years in the fishing port of Macduff, Banffshire, on the Moray Firth and was a leading expert on the fisherfolk of Scotland. He wrote many books dealing with the sea, ships and sailing, but his main interest was in the east-coast fishermen, about whom he wrote this work in 1950. (Another of his many books is entitled *Fishing Boats and Fishing Folk on the East Coast of Scotland*.) Anson was also a distinguished artist, and illustrated his own books.

There were lucky and unlucky boats. Some were believed to have an unlucky 'spehl' in them. Shipwrights would claim to foretell the luck of a boat by the way in which a certain 'spehl,' or chip of wood, came off when they began work on the building. At Nairn, it was a saying that a boat built of 'she-wood' sailed faster by night than by day. To bring good luck to a new boat, the owner's wife had to put on the first 'mop' of tar — at least such was a superstition at Portknockie.

Both on the East and on the West coasts, fishermen believed that a boat must always be rowed sunways when first leaving the shore. At Buckie, and in other places, it was regarded as tempting providence to turn a boat in harbour against the sun. The saying was: 'Pit the boatie's heid wast aboot.'

When a new boat was brought back to Crovie for the first time, those who were to do so had to set out when the tide was 'flouwin''. On the arrival of the boat, the villagers would meet her on the shore. Bread, cheese, beer or whisky were given to all. A glass of beer or spirits had to be broken over the boat, with the following 'blessing' or similar words: 'I wiss this ane may gyang as lan safe oot an' in, an' catch as mony fish as the aul' ane.' It was considered unlucky to go for a new boat and return without her.

At Portessie the fisher folk used to gather round a new boat. One of them would throw beer over her, sing out her name, and the onlookers cheered. Then followed the 'boat feast,' with beer, cheese, whisky or porter — a dinner of broth, beef, and plenty of whisky.

The superstition about flowing tides also affected other incidents of the fishing besides boats. When a new line was made, the job had to be

started only on an outgoing tide, and continued without any interruption. At Portessie the first person entering a house where a 'greatline' was being made had to pay for a mutchkin of whisky, to be drunk in the house after the line was finished. But the line itself got the first glass; the whisky being poured over it.

In the larger fishing boats of the middle of the last century, the crew usually consisted of eight men, each of whom had their distinctive name. Those in the bow were known as 'hanksmen.' At a 'boat feast' all sat together as they would be at sea. Drinking was often carried on throughout the night. A common toast was:

> 'Health t' men, an' death t' fish,
> They're waggin' their tails, it'll pay for this.'

Scots Fisherfolk

Anonymous

Alan MacLean

This anonymous nineteenth-century folk song was among those gathered up by that great collector of north-east ballads, Gavin Greig. It can be found in *Folk Songs of the North East* by Gavin Greig, edited by Kenneth Goldstein and Arthur Argo, published by Folklore Associates.

I was born in Cullen,
    A minister's son,
Brocht up wi' gweed learnin'
    Till my school-days were done.

I went to the College
    A student to be,
But the marriage at Westfield
    Has quite ruined me.

There was Grant and Mackenzie,
    Macdonald and I,
And we went to the weddin'
    Pretty girls for to spy.

We danced and we sang
    And we took great delight,
And bonnie Sally Allan
    Cam oft in my sight.

'O Sally, dear Sally,
    Will you take a dram?'
'O yes, my dear Alan,
    If it comes from your hand.'

I gied her a dance
    And I gied her a dram,
And I asked her quite kindly
    If she'd go to the broom.

She disliked my offer
    But gave the least froon.
Says she, 'My dear Alan,
    Had it been my doom.'

So we went to the broom
    In the middle o' the night;
We had neither coal nor candle
    But the moon gave us light.

But her father next morning
    To the College he came;
He was all in a passion
    At Alan MacLean.

'If it's true,' says the Regent,
    'As I fear it's no lie,
This day from Aulton College
    Young Alan must fly.'

'Tomorrow's the graduation
    And Tuesday's the Ball,
But we'll banish young Alan
    From the Aulton College Hall.'

My father's a minister,
    He preaches at Tain.
My mother died in the Hielands
    And I daurna gae hame.

It's I intended a minister
    But that winna do;
It's now for a doctor
    That I maun pursue.

Prince Charles the Royal
    Lies out in the bay,
Takin' on goods and passengers
    And she'll surely take me.

Fare ye weel, Aulton College,
    Likewise Aberdeen.
Fare ye weel, Sally Allan,
    Who lives by yon green.

If ever I return again,
    As I hope that I shall,
We will have a merry bottle
    Near the Aulton College Hall.

Ay, if ever I return again,
  As I hope that I shall,
I will marry Sally Allan
  In spite o' them all.

Folk Songs of the North East

Very fou

George IV in Scotland, 1822

The King's Dram

1.

About noon of the 14th of August, the royal yacht and the attendant vessels of war cast anchor in the Roads of Leith; but although Scott's ballad-prologue had entreated the clergy to 'warstle for a sunny day,' the weather was so unpropitious that it was found necessary to defer the landing until the 15th. In the midst of the rain, however, Sir Walter rowed off to the Royal George, and, says the newspaper of the day, —

'When his arrival alongside the yacht was announced to the King, — "What!" exclaimed his Majesty, "Sir Walter Scott! The man in Scotland I most wish to see! Let him come up." This distinguished Baronet then ascended the ship, and was presented to the King on the quarter-deck, where, after an appropriate speech in name of the ladies of Edinburgh, he presented his Majesty with a St Andrew's Cross, in silver, which his fair subjects had provided for him. The King, with evident marks of satisfaction, made a gracious reply to Sir Walter, received the gift in the most kind and condescending manner, and promised to wear it in public, in token of acknowledgment to the fair donors.'

To this record let me add, that, on receiving the poet on the quarter-deck, his Majesty called for a bottle of Highland whisky, and having drunk his health in this national liquor, desired a glass to be filled for him. Sir Walter, after draining his own bumper, made a request that the King would condescend to bestow on him the glass out of which his Majesty had just drunk his health; and this being granted, the precious vessel was immediately wrapped up and carefully deposited in what he conceived to be the safest part of his dress. So he returned with it to Castle Street; but — to say nothing at this moment of graver distractions — on reaching his house he found a guest established there of a sort rather different from the usual visiters of the time. The poet Crabbe, to whom he had been introduced when last in London by Mr Murray of Albemarle Street, after repeatedly promising to follow up the acquaintance by an excursion to the north, had at last arrived in the midst of these tumultuous preparations for the royal advent. Notwithstanding all such impediments, he found his quarters ready for him, and Scott entering,

wet and hurried, embraced the venerable man with brotherly affection. The royal gift was forgotten — the ample skirt of the coat within which it had been packed, and which he had hitherto held cautiously in front of his person, slipped back to its more usual position — he sat down beside Crabbe, and the glass was crushed to atoms. His scream and gesture made his wife conclude that he had sat down on a pair of scissors, or the like; but very little harm had been done except the breaking of the glass, of which alone he had been thinking. This was a damage not to be repaired: as for the scratch that accompanied it, its scar was of no great consequence, as even when mounting the 'cat-dath, or battle-garment' of the Celtic Club, he adhered, like his hero Waverley, to *the trews.*

J.G. Lockhart, *The Life of Sir Walter Scott*

2.

This autumn King George the Fourth visited Scotland. The whole country went mad. Everybody strained every point to get to Edinburgh to receive him. Sir Walter Scott and the Town Council were overwhelming themselves with the preparations. My mother did not feel well enough for the bustle, neither was I at all fit for it, so we stayed at home with aunt Mary. My father, my sisters and William, with lace, feathers, pearls, the old landau, the old horses, and the old liveries, all went to add to the show, which they said was delightful. The Countess of Lauderdale presented my two sisters and the two Miss Grants of Congalton, a group allowed to be the prettiest there. The Clan Grant had quite a triumph, no equipage was as handsome as that of Colonel Francis Grant, our acting chief, in their red and green and gold. There were processions, a review, a levée, a drawing-room, and a ball, at which last Jane was one of the ladies selected to dance in the reel before the King, with, I think, poor Captain Murray of Abercairney, a young naval officer, for her partner. A great mistake was made by the stage managers — one that offended all the southron Scots; the King wore at the levée the Highland dress. I daresay he thought the country all Highland, expected no fertile plains, did not know the difference between the Saxon and the Celt. However, all else went off well, this little slur on the Saxon was overlooked, and it gave occasion for a laugh at one of Lady Saltoun's witty speeches. Some one objecting to this dress, particularly on so large a man, 'Nay,' said she, 'we should take it very kind of him; since his stay will be so short, the more we see of him the better.' Sir William Curtis was kilted too, and standing near the King, many persons mistook them, amongst others John Hamilton Dundas, who kneeled to kiss the fat Alderman's hand, when, finding out his mistake, he called, 'Wrong, by Jove!' and rising, moved on undaunted to the larger presence. One incident connected with this time made me very cross. Lord Conyngham, the Chamberlain, was looking everywhere for pure Glenlivet whisky; the King drank nothing else. It was not to be had out of the Highlands. My father sent word to me — I was the cellarer — to empty my pet bin, where was whisky long in wood, long in uncorked bottles, mild as milk, and the true contraband *goût* in it. Much as I grudged this treasure it made our fortunes afterwards, showing on what trifles great events depend. The whisky, and fifty brace of ptarmigan all shot by one man, went up to Holyrood House, and were graciously received and made much of, and a reminder of this attention at a proper moment by the gentlemanly Chamberlain ensured to my father the Indian judgeship.

Elizabeth Grant of Rothiemurchus, *Memoirs of a Highland Lady*

D. MacLeod Malloch

The Reformed Dram-Shop

In the preface to this book of anecdotes, published in 1912, the author wrote that it: 'deals with anecdotes as distinguished from history.' He added that 'much will be found in it that is interesting and amusing, and he therefore hopes that the book will prove acceptable to all who are interested in the welfare of the City of Glasgow.'

Mr James Smith tried, by opening a temperance coffee-house in Jail Square, to minimise some of the drinking habits. Below is given a copy of its announcement written by 'Sandy M'Alpine' (the late William Walker):—

A WONDER, A WONDER, A WONDER FOR TO SEE!
A BRAW COFFEE-HOOSE WHAUR A DRAM-SHOP USED
TO BE!
FREENS
AN' FELLOW-CEETIZENS
IN GENERAL!
AN' YOU FOKE ABOOT THE FUT O' THE SAUTMARKET IN
PARTIK'LAR
WILL YE SPEAK A WORD WI' ME?

I'm an auld WHISKY-SHOP; I'm an interestin' relick o' anshient times, and mainners. Maybe sum o' ye dinna ken what a Whisky-shop is. I'll tell ye.

In anshient times — lang before puir Workin' Foke were sae wise or weel daein' as they are noo-a-days — the Gleska Foke, an' partik'larly the Foke aboot the fut o' the SAUTMARKET, were awfu' fond o' WHISKY. This WHISKY was a sort o' DEEVIL'S DRINK, made out o' GOD'S gude BARLEY.

It robbit men o' their judgment; but they drank it.
It robbit them o' their nait'ral affeckshun; but they drank it.
It robbit them o' independence an' self respeck; but they drank it.
It made them mean, unmanly, disgustin' wretches; but they drank it.

It made them savage an' quarrelsome; but they drank it.

It cled them wi' rags; but they drank it.

It made them live in low, filthy dens o' hooses; but they drank it.

It sent them in scores to the Poleece Office; but they drank it.

It sent them to Jail, the Hulks, an' the Gallows; but they drank it.

Bailies an' Sherrifs, Judges an' Justices, deplored its effecks; but they drank it themsel's!

Ministers preached aboot it; but they drank it themsel's!

It blottit oot God's glorious image frae men's faces an' hearts; but they drank it.

It made them beggars; but they drank it.

It made them paupers; but they drank it.

It made them idiots; but they drank it.

This WHISKY, then, wuz selt in Shops, an' I wuz ane o' them, — That'll let ye ken what a Whisky-Shop wuz in anshient times. TIMES ARE CHANGED NOO. Every body's a member o' the Scottish Temperance-League; naebody drinks onything but Coffee; so I've ta'en up the Coffee-House line mysel'!

Come and see me! Ye'll get Rowsin' Cups o' Coffee! Thumpin' Cups o' Tea! Thund'rin' Dunts o'Bread! Whangs o' Cheese! Lots o' Ham an' Eggs, Staiks, Chops, an a' ither kinds o' Substanshials!

FREENS AN' FELLOW-CEETIZENS. — I'm no'the Shop I ance wuz. I've a blythe heart an'a cheery face noo. Come an' see me!

THE REFORMED
DRAM SHOP,
20 JAIL SQUARE.

OBSERVE. — Nae Connexion wi' the JAIL owre the way.

The Fair, now, is essentially for the benefit of the working classes, and is keenly enjoyed by them. It is something outside the daily round of possible amusements. Unfortunately the public-house enters very largely into the life of the Glasgow labouring classes, and seemingly a considerable pleasure is derived from actual drunkenness. At least that is the conclusion one must draw from the fact that the patrons of the public-houses deliberately order whatever compound (such as beer and whisky) they know will speedily produce intoxication. Others with equal deliberation set out for a prolonged bout of drunkenness. While this sort of thing is a blot on the fair fame of the City, it occasionally has an amusing side. As an example of the 'spree deliberate,' one may cite the case of John Smith, a quay labourer, but a man of family and some time a man of substance in Wales. To him fell a legacy of a thousand pounds one day; and his way of spending it could only have found proper sympathy at the quay. It was most simple. He placed his wife and three children inside one of the old quayside growlers, and the legatee sat himself on the box beside the driver. At every tavern they stopped, and the driver brought out drinks. Smith drank on the box, his wife in the cab, and the driver on the street. And so to the next one. Then home in the evening, hallooing along the quayside, to the delight of the neighbourhood. He did not forget past days, but lent money lavishly, and filled the lumpers so 'fou' that a boat missed the tide, and the whole shed was demoralised for weeks. A short life, but a merry one, my masters. First, the old horse, sickened with perplexity as to when the fare would end, dropped off after ten weeks of it. Then, and just before the old driver was about to follow, − reluctant as he was now that life had at last blossomed to him, − the thousand pounds ran out; the last twenty going to pay for a chemist's shop which Mr Smith wrecked to express disapproval of the doctor's not wearing his tall hat while he called on his wife.

A week later John Smith, Esquire, became 'Jake' once more, bending his broad back in the trucks without a single show of regret. And his wife, although she missed her outings, seems not unreconciled to her lot as long as her husband can sport of a Sunday his Newmarket coat and blue waistcoat as outward and visible signs that they were carriage folk in their day.

The Book of Glasgow Anecdote

James Hogg

Enchanted Drinking

James Hogg (1770−1835) drew on Border folklore for much of the material of his poetry and fiction. Until fairly recently regarded somewhat patronisingly as 'the Ettrick Shepherd', Hogg is now increasingly recognised as one of the greatest figures in Scottish literature.

He can turn a man into a boy;
    A boy into an ass;
He can change your gold into white moneye;
    Your white moneye into brass;
He can turn our goodman to a beast
    With hoof, but, an' with horn,
And chap the goodwife in her cheer,
    This little John Barleycorn.

Old Song

The plan of our great necromancer was no other than that of pushing round the wine, and other strong intoxicating liquors, to the utmost extremity; and it is well known that these stimulating beverages have charms that no warrior, or other person accustomed to violent exertions, can withstand, after indulging in them to a certain extent. The mirth and argument, or rather the bragg of weir, grew first obstreperous, afterwards boisterous and unruly, and several of the men got up and strode the hall with drawn swords, without being able to tell with whom they were offended or going to fight. Neither the Master nor the abbot discouraged this turmoil, but pushed round the liquor, till some of the most intimate friends and associates of the party, in the extravagance of intoxication, actually wounded one another, and afterwards blubbered, like children, for vexation. While they were all in this state of unnatural elevation, father Lawrence got up, and addressed himself to the party, for the first time. He represented to them, by striking metaphors, the uncertainty and toil of the warrior's life; and requested all such of them as loved ease, freedom, and independence, to become inmates of his habitation; and during the time of their noviciates, he promised them every good thing. Several of them pretended to snap at the proffer, some on one condition, some on another; but when he presented a scroll of parchment, written in red characters, for their marks or signatures, no one would sign and seal, save Tam Craik, who put his mark to it three times with uncommon avidity, on the positive condition that he was to have as much fat flesh as he could eat for the first three years, at all times that he chose, by day or by night.

When matters were at this pass, and our brave yeomen could with difficulty rise to their feet, they heard a chorus of sweet and melodious music approaching, which still drew nearer and nearer. This was a treat they little expected in such an habitation; but how much greater was their surprise, when the hall-door was thrown open, and there were ushered in thirty of the most lovely maidens that the eyes of men had ever beheld. They seemed, too, to be all of noble lineage, for they were dressed like eastern princesses, rustling in their silks, and covered over with dazzling gems. The Master welcomed them with stately courtesy, apologizing for the state of his castle, and the necessity they would be under of sitting down and sharing the feast with warriors, who, however, he assured them were all gallant gentlemen, of his own kin, and some of them of his own name. The splendid dames answered that nothing on earth would give them so much delight as to share the feast with gentlemen and warriors, the natural protectors of their helpless sex, to whom it should be their principal aim to pay all manner of deference.

As soon as the door was opened, our brave yeomen, with the profound respect that men of their boisterous occupation always pay to female beauty and rare accomplishments, started all to their feet, and made their obeisance. But the worst concern for them was, that they could not stand on their feet. Some of them propped themselves on the hilts of their sheathed swords, leaning the points backward against the wall. Others kept a sly hold of the buff-belt of the comrade next to him; and a few, of whom the poet was one, and Tam another, lost their balance, and fell back over the benches, showing the noble dames the soles of their sandals. All was silence and restraint, and a view of no group could be more amusing; for though our heroes were hardly able to behave themselves with the utmost propriety, yet they were all endeavouring to do it; some keeping their mouths close shut, that no misbecoming word might possibly escape from their lips; some turning up their white faces, manifesting evident symptoms of sickness, and some unable to refrain their joy at this grand addition to their party.

The first breaking up of the conversation was likewise extremely curious; but it was begun in so many corners about the same time, it is impossible to detail it all. Will Martin, with a lisping unbowsome tongue, addressed the one next to him to the following effect.

'Fine evening this, noble dame.'

'Do you account this so very fine an evening, gallant knight?'

'Hem, Hem; glorious roads too; most noble lady, — paced all with — marble, you know. Hem! Came you by the marble path, fair lady? Hem! hem!'

'Not by the marble path, most courteous knight, but on one of alabaster, bordered with emeralds, rubies, and diamonds you know. Hem! hem!'

'May all the powers — Hem — powers of beauty, you know — Ay — hem! and love. Hem! What was I about to say?'

'Could not guess, knight.'

'That smile is so sweet. Will such an — hem! — such an angelic creature, — really con — descend to converse familiarly with a plain, homely warrior?'

'Your notice does me far too much honour, worthy knight.' And so saying she put the tip of her palm gently on the warrior's rough hand. Intoxicated as Will was with wine, he was petrified with astonishment and delight, and could not find terms to express his gratitude and adoration. Many others were likewise by the same time testifying, by their bright and exulting looks, the joy and delight they were experiencing in the conversation of those most beautiful and refined of all earthly objects. Tam Craik beheld, or thought he beheld, his lovely Kell among them, blooming in tenfold loveliness. He was so drunk that he could not articulate one syllable; but he fixed his long coulter-nose and grey eyes steadily in the direction of her face, and put his hand below the table and scratched.

Still the cup and the cates circulated without any respite. The Master and the abbot both called them round and round; and though the lovely and high-born dames tasted sparingly, nevertheless the circumstances of

157

their having touched the cup with their lips was sufficient to induce the enamoured warriors to drink to them in healths deep and dangerous. Reason had long been tottering on her throne with the best of them, but these amorous draughts of homage overthrew her completely, and laid her grovelling in the dust. The heroes fell from their seats first by ones, but ere the last in threes and fours. Still the courteous and sympathetic beauties tried to administer comfort and assistance to their *natural protectors*, by holding up their heads, and chafing their temples; but, in spite of all they could do, total oblivion of passing events ensued to the whole of our incautious troopers.

The next morning presented a scene in the great hall of Aikwood, which, if it cannot be described, neither can it ever be conceived. There lay our troop of gallant yeomen, as good as ever heaved buckler, scattered over the floor; some in corners, some below benches, every one of their eyes sealed in profound slumber though the day was well advanced, and every one having an inamorata in his arms, or clinging close to him of her own accord. At a given signal, the great bell of the castle was rung with a knell that might have wakened the dead. The sleepers raised their drowsy and aching heads all at the same time: and, as was natural, every one turned his eyes first toward the partner of his slumbers. Their sensations may be in some measure conceived, when, instead of the youthful, blooming, angelic beings, whom they had seen over-night, there lay a group of the most horrible hags that ever opened eyes on the light of day. Instead of the light, flowing, and curled hair, there hung portions of grey dishevelled locks. Instead of the virgin bloom of the cheek, and the brilliant enamel of the eye, all was rheum, haggardness, and deformity. Some had two or three long pitted teeth, of the colour of amber; some had none. Their lovely mouths were adorned with curled and silvery mustachios; and their fair necks were shrivelled and seriated like the bark of a pine-tree. Instead of the rustling silks and dazzling jewels, they were all clothed in noisome rags; and, to crown the horror of our benumbed and degraded Bacchanalians, every one of the witches had her eyes fixed on her partner, gleaming with hellish delight at the state to which they had reduced themselves, and the horrors of their feelings. The poet, and two or three others, fell into convulsions; and all of them turned away groaning, and hid their faces from these objects of abhorrence.

The Three Perils of Man

A Fatal Necessity

Character. — A sense of religion and decency prevails among the people in general. One man only, within the memory of tradition, was convicted of a capital crime, and suffered for it about 50 years ago. No doubt, such a number engaged in distilling spirits, has a tendency to corrupt the morals, but the bad effects of this trade are less discernible than might be feared. Were the effects worse than they are, there is a fatal necessity of continuing the distillery, until some other manufacture be established in its stead, whereby the people will be enabled to find money to pay their rents. The worst effect of the great plenty of spirits is, that dram shops are set up almost in every village for retail, where young and idle people convene and get drunk. These tipling huts are kept by such only as are not able to pay a fine, or procure a licence. They are the greatest nuisance in the parish. It is a pity that no effectual mode has as yet been projected for suppressing them.

Statistical Account of Scotland, VII (Parish of Urray, Counties of Ross and Inverness), 1793

Keeping The King's Birthday in the Eighteenth Century

1.

Friday last, being the anniversary of his majesty's [*George III*] birth-day, when he entered into the 36th year of his age, was observed here with the greatest demonstrations of joy. In the morning the flag was displayed from the castle, at noon there was a round of the great guns, returned by three vollies from a party of the military drawn up on the Castle-hill, and accompanied by the ringing of the music-bells. About four in the afternoon, the lord provost, magistrates and council, attended by a number of noblemen and gentlemen, specially invited, with the officers of the army and trained-bands, assembled in the Parliament-house, where they drank the health of the day, and a variety of loyal toasts, announced by the flourish of trumpets, and vollies of small arms from the city-guard, drawn up in the Parliament close. After which the evening concluded with a brilliant assembly. — It is, however, to be regretted, that, on such days of festivity, the lower class of people seldom indulge their mirth without mischief. On this occasion they became, towards the evening, perfectly licentious, and, after their ammunition of squibs and crackers was exhausted, they employed dead cats, mud &c. which they discharged very plentifully on the city guard; and, when threatened to be chastised or apprehended, they betook themselves to the more dangerous weapons of stones and brickbats, &c. In this encounter several of the guard were wounded, and they in return dealt their blows pretty liberally, by which, amid the confusion, some innocent persons suffered along with the guilty. A number of young lads, suspected of having been concerned in the riot, were apprehended; but most of them were set at liberty next morning, by their friends becoming bail for their appearance when called. Five of the most active were committed to the tolbooth, upon application of the procurator fiscal, and still remain there where they will have time to repent of their folly in cool blood.

The Weekly Magazine or Edinburgh Amusement, 10 June 1773

2.

Another [*test of loyalty*] was *keeping* the King's birth-day. This day was the 4th of June, which for the 60 years that the reign of George the III lasted gave an annual holiday to the British people, and was so associated in their habits with the idea of its being a free day, that they thought they had a right to it even after his Majesty was dead. And the established way of keeping it in Edinburgh was, by the lower orders and the boys having a long day of idleness and fire-works, and by the upper classes going to the Parliament House, and drinking the royal health in the evening, at the expense of the city funds. The magistrates who conducted the banquet, which began about seven, invited about 1500 people. Tables, but no seats except one at each end, were set along the Outer House. These tables, and the doors and walls, were adorned by flowers and branches, the trampling and bruising of which increased the general filth. There was no silence, no order, no decency. The loyal toasts were let off, in all quarters, according to the pleasure of the Town Councillor who presided over the section, without any orations by the Provost, who, seated in his robes, on a high chair, was supposed to control the chaos. Respectable people, considering it all an odious penance, and going merely in order to shew that they were not Jacobins, came away after having pretended to drink one necessary cup to the health of the reigning monarch. But all sorts who were worthy of the occasion and enjoyed it, persevered to a late hour, roaring, drinking, toasting, and quarrelling. They made the Court stink for a week with the wreck and the fumes of that hot and scandalous night. It was not unusual at old Scotch feasts for the guests, after drinking a toast, to toss their glasses over their heads, in order that they might never be debased by any other sentiment. The very loyal on this occasion availed themselves of this privilege freely, so that fragments of glass crunched beneath the feet of the walkers. The infernal din was aggravated by volleys of musketry, fired very awkwardly by the Town Guard, amidst the shouts of the mob, in the Parliament Close. The rabble, smitten by the enthusiasm of the day, were accustomed, and permitted, to think license their right, and exercised their brutality without stint. Those who were aware of what might take place on the street, retired from the banquet before the spirit of mischief was fully up. Those who came out so late as ten or even nine of the evening, if observed and unprotected, were fortunate if they escaped rough usage, especially if they escaped being 'Burghered', or made to 'Ride the Stang', a painful and dangerous operation, and therefore a great favourite with the mob. I forget when this abominable festival was given up. Not, I believe, till the poverty, rather than the will, of the Town Council was obliged to consent.

Lord Cockburn, *Memorials of His Time*

William McIlvanney

In The Red Lion

The novel from which this extract is taken was published in 1985,
and is set in a decaying community in an Ayrshire town. McIlvanney
is a leading figure in the 'new realist' school of Scottish fiction.

The sign of the Red Lion had rebounded on itself a bit, like a statement
to which subsequent circumstances have given an ironic significance. It
seemed meant to be a lion rampant. But the projecting rod of metal to
which the sign was fixed by two cleeks had buckled in some forgotten
storm. The lion that had been rearing so proudly now looked as if it
were in the process of lying down or even hiding, and exposure to rough
weather appeared to have given it the mange.

That image of a defiant posture being beaten down was appropriate.
The place still called itself a hotel, although the only two rooms that
were kept in readiness stood nearly every night in stillness, ghostly
with clean white bed-linen, shrines to the unknown traveller. The small
dining-room was seldom used, since pub lunches were the only meals
ever in demand. The Red Lion scavenged a lean life from the takings of
the public bar.

Like alcohol for a terminal alcoholic, the bar was both the means of
the hotel's survival and the guarantee that it couldn't survive much
longer. It seemed helplessly set in its ways, making no attempt to adapt
itself to a changing situation. There were no fruit-machines, no space-
invaders. There was a long wooden counter. There were some wooden
tables and wooden chairs set out across a wide expanse of fraying carpet.
There was, dominating a room that could feel as large as a church when
empty, the big gantry like an organ for the evocation of pagan moods.
Quite a few empty optics suggested that the range of evocation now
possible was not what it had been.

It had its regulars but they were mainly upwards of their thirties and
there weren't many women among them. Except for occasional freak
nights when the pub was busy and briefly achieved a more complicated
sense of itself the way a person might when on holiday, its procedures
were of a pattern. The people who came here were, after all, devotees of
a dying tradition. They believed in pubs as they had been in the past
and they came here simply to drink and talk among friends, refresh small

163

dreams and opinionate on matters of national importance. It was a talking shop where people used conversation the way South American peasants chew coca leaves, to keep out the cold.

Most of the men who drank in the Red Lion couldn't afford to drink much. Sometimes a pint took so long to go down you might have imagined each mouthful had to be chewed before it was swallowed. They had all known better times and were fearing worse. The room they stood in was proof of how bad things were. It was common talk that Alan Morrison's hold on the premises was shaky and every other week, as the property mouldered around him, another rumour of the brewers buying him out blew through it like a draught. The more uncertain his tenure grew to be, the more determinedly his regulars came. It was a small warmth in their lives and they were like men reluctant to abandon their places round a fire, though they know it's going out.

Alan Morrison shared their feeling. He was simply holding out as long as he could. He knew that his monthly accounts were an unanswerable argument, but buying the hotel twenty years ago, after years of careful saving, had never been primarily an act of commercial logic. It had been the fulfilment of a dream for him and, being a stubborn man, he simply refused to wake up, though these days it was taking more and more whisky to keep him like that. For a while, knowing how badly things were going and lacking sufficient belief in new ways to change, he had settled for being a pedant of his own condition, a theorist about why things were so bad.

At one time he had blamed the Miners' Welfare Club. Everybody wanted to be a capitalist, he said. When that closed down, he decided that television was the cause. People sat at home drinking out of cans, he said. That annoyed him for a while. Some evenings in the quietness of the pub, he would stand with an abstracted air, tuned out of whatever muffled conversation was taking place, as if listening for the chorus of beer cans hissing open in all the houses of the town. When the television set he installed in the bar didn't help, he retired further into his whisky for deeper contemplation of the problem.

The answer he came out with was an old man's frozen reflex to the changes in the world, not so much a rational process as a mental snarl, the rictus of an animal that has died trying to intimidate the trap which has caught it. He became a kind of King Lear with a hotel, dismissive of all the world except his clientele. The commercial failure of his hotel wasn't the reason for his baffled anger, merely its rostrum. His wife had died of cancer. His only son emigrated. His own heart was giving out. The state of his trade was just external confirmation, like an official letter from the fates.

His son became his scapegoat. Alan Morrison somehow managed to hallucinate a great inheritance for his son if he hadn't gone to Australia. If he had stayed, everything would have been all right. The reason for

Alec's going became in his father's mind something that he had caused. From there it was but a short tirade to Alan's main theme, a sweeping dismissal of the young. They loved going to loud places. 'Noise isny meaning' was one of his darker utterances. They smoked strange cigarettes in groups. He would talk of the dangers of such practices while he was downing a double whisky. It was as if they, too, had emigrated, not geographically but socially, to other customs, to new attitudes, to more exotic pleasures.

Like his son, they never came regularly to his place, except for one. Vince Mabon was a student. 'Politics' was his cryptic answer to anyone in the bar who asked him what he was studying. He often said it with a cupping gesture of his hands that seemed to imply a casual encompassing of the world and all it might contain. Vince had a kind of deliberate intensity, a way of turning forensically into any question, even if you were asking him the time. No conversation seemed trivial with him. He always gave the impression of being on a mission of some sort. He didn't drink here so much as he came among them.

He was in the bar that Sunday. He had explained to nobody in particular that, as he had no lectures the next morning, he had managed to stay in Thornbank another night. The news was received without a display of fireworks. The only others present at the time, besides old Alan behind the bar, were the three domino players and Fast Frankie White.

The domino players were always looking for a fourth because as purists they hated sleeping dominoes. With not all the dominoes in use, arguments frequently broke out among them, arguments that almost always came back to theatrical complaints about the impossibility of deploying the full complexity of their skills when not every domino was brought into play. They sounded like Grand Masters being asked to play without the queen. Tonight there seemed no possibility of their artistry being given full range. Alan was engaged in trying to get Vince Mabon to admit the folly of being young. Fast Frankie White was drinking with his customary self-consciousness, as if checking the camera-angles.

He was an outsider in his home town, Frankie White, and perhaps everywhere. Nobody was even sure where the nickname 'Fast' had come from, maybe from the publicity agent he carried around in his head. Most people in Thornbank knew that whatever he did it wasn't strictly legal. But since they knew of nobody he had harmed, except for breaking his mother's heart (and what son didn't?), they tolerated him. He might be able to sell the image he had made of himself elsewhere but they knew him too well to take him seriously. He was a performance and they let it happen, as long as it didn't interfere significantly with them. Tonight he had kept to himself, drinking his whisky with a nervous expectation, and seeming to listen with sophisticated amusement to Vince and Alan.

Vince's mushroom hairstyle was nodding heatedly at Alan and he had spilled some of his light beer on his UCLA tee-shirt. Alan was holding his whisky glass to the optic and shaking his head.

'Well, I wouldn't go, anyway,' Vince said. 'And that's for sure.'

'But they're payin' his way,' Alan said, and dropped a token bead of water in his glass. 'The whole trip won't cost him a penny.'

'Doesn't matter. Doesn't matter.'

'It's his son and his wife, for God's sake. Bert's got two grand-daughters out there he's never even seen.'

'His son could bring them over.'

'It's not like he's goin' to *stay* in South Africa. Ah could see the force of yer objections then. It's just a holiday.'

'He's still sanctioning an oppressive regime,' Vince said.

Alan emptied an ashtray that had nothing in it, wiped it with a cloth that made it slightly less clean and replaced it on the bar. He looked at his glass for advice.

'You ever been to Prestwick for the day?' he asked.

'What?'

'You ever been to Prestwick for the day?'

Vince looked round, appealing to a non-existent public. He smiled to himself since nobody else was available.

'I think that's what they call a non sequitur, Alan,' he said.

'That's maybe what you call it. Ah just call it a question. Fuckin' answer it.'

'Yes. Guilty. I've been to Prestwick for the day. A lot of times.'

'Well. Don't go again. It's a Tory council.'

The Big Man

(From the Greenock Advertiser)

Disgraceful Wrecking Scenes at Islay

The brig Mary Ann, of Greenock, now lying a wreck at Kilchoman Bay, Islay, is fast breaking up, and portions of the cargo floating ashore. Up to Saturday there had been about 200 boxes saved, containing bottled brandy, whisky, and gin, and upwards of six puncheons of whisky, brandy, and wine; but the wildest scenes of drunkenness and riot that can be imagined took place. Hundreds of people flocked from all parts of the neighbourhood, especially the Portnahaven fishermen, who turned out to a man. Boxes were seized as soon as landed, broken up, and the

contents carried away and drunk. Numbers could be seen here and there lying amongst the rocks, unable to move, while others were fighting like savages. Sergeant Kennedy and constable Chisholm, of the County Police, were in attendance, and used every means in their power to put a stop to the work of pillage. They succeeded in keeping some order during the day of Thursday, but when night came on the natives showed evident symptoms of their disapproval of the police being there at all, and on the latter preventing a fellow from knocking the end out of a puncheon, in order, as he said, to 'treat all hands,' they were immediately seized upon by the mob, and a hand-to-hand fight ensued, which lasted half an hour, and ended in the defeat of the police, of whom there were only two against from 30 to 40 of the natives. The police beat a retreat to Cuil Farm — about a mile from the scene of action — closely pursued by about 30 of the natives, yelling like savages. Mrs Simpson of Cuil, on seeing the state of matters, took the police into the house and secured the doors, at the same time placing arms at their disposal for their protection. The mob yelled two or three times round the house, but learning that the police had got fire-arms, they left and returned to the beach. Next morning the scene presented was still more frightful to contemplate. In one place there lay stretched the dead body of a large and powerful man, Donald M'Phayden, a fisherman from Portnahaven, who was considered the strongest man in Islay; but the brandy proved to be still stronger. He has left a wife and family. Others apparently in a dying state were being conveyed to the nearest houses, where every means were used to save life. Mrs Simpson, who is a very kind and humane person, supplied every remedy, but there was no medical man within fifteen or sixteen miles of the place. Mr James Simpson got a coffin made for M'Phayden, and had him interred on Friday. At the time when the corpse was being taken away, some groups could be seen fighting, others dancing, and others craving for drink, in order, as they said, to bury the man decently. Up to Saturday there was only one death, but it was reported on Monday that two more had died. The Mary Ann had on board 300 tons of pig-iron, a large quantity of spirits, and other general cargo, from Glasgow to New Brunswick. Shortly after going to sea, she became leaky, put into Dublin, where she discharged, and got repaired. Going to sea again, she sprang a leak off the west coast of Islay, the wind blowing fresh off the land; and Captain Pryce, finding the vessel in a sinking state and quite unmanageable, along with the crew, abandoned the vessel. The wind veering round to the westward, a fisherman picked her up and ran into Kilchoman Bay, where she sank in shallow water.

Argyllshire Herald, 27 May 1859

J.G. Lockhart

A Burns Supper, 1817

John Gibson Lockhart (1794–1854), Sir Walter Scott's son-in-law and biographer, here describes a Burns supper in Edinburgh at which James Hogg, 'the Ettrick Shepherd' and John Wilson, 'Christopher North', were present.

In process of time, the less jovial members of the company began to effect their retreat, and the Laird and I, espying some vacant places at the table where Mr Wilson and the Ettrick Shepherd were seated, were induced to shift our situation, for the sake of being nearer these celebrated characters. I was placed within a few feet of Hogg, and introduced to Wilson across the table, and soon found, from the way in which the bottle circulated in this quarter, that both of them inherited in perfection the old feud of Burns against the '*aquae potores.*' As to the bottle, indeed, I should exclude Hogg; for he, long before I came into his neighbourhood, had finished the bottle of port allowed by our traiteur, and was deep in a huge jug of whisky toddy — in the manufacture of which he is supposed to excel almost as much as Burns did — and in its consumption too, although happily in rather a more moderate degree.

After this time, I suspect the prescribed order of toasts began to be sadly neglected, for long speeches were uttered from remote corners, nobody knew by whom or about what; song after song was volunteered; and all the cold restraints of sobriety being gradually thawed by the sun of festive cheer.

> Wit walked the rounds, and music filled the air.

The inimitable 'Jolly Beggars' of the poet, which has lately been set to music, was got up in high style, the songs being exquisitely sung by Messrs Swift, Templeton, and Lees, and the recitative read with much effect by Mr B——. But even this entertainment, with all its inherent variety, was too regular for the taste of the assembly. The chairman himself broke in upon it the first, by proposing a very appropriate toast, which I shall attempt to naturalize in Cardiganshire; this again called up a very old gentleman, who conceived that some compliment had been intended for a club of which he is president; in short, compliments and toasts became so interlaced and interlarded, that nobody could think of taking up the thread of 'The Jolly Beggars' again. By the way, this inimitable Cantata is not to be found in Currie's edition, and I suspect you are a stranger even to its name; and yet, had Burns left nothing more than this behind him, I think he would still have left enough to justify all the honour in which his genius is held. There does not exist, in any one piece throughout the whole range of English poetry, such a collection of true, fresh, and characteristic lyrics. Here we have nothing, indeed, that is very high, but we have much that is very tender. What can be better in its way, than the fine song of the Highland Widow, 'wha had in mony a well been douked?' . . .

A man may now and then, adopt a change of liquor with advantage; but, upon the whole, I like better to see people 'stick to their vocation.' I think nothing can be a more pitiable sight than a French count on his travels, striving to look pleased over a bumper of strong Port; and an Oxford doctor of divinity looks almost as much like a fish out of water, when he is constrained to put up with the best Claret in the world. In like manner, it would have tended very much to disturb my notions of propriety, had I found Hogg drinking Hock. It would have been a sin against *keeping* with such a face as he has. Although for some time past he has spent a considerable portion of every year in excellent, even in refined society, the external appearance of the man can have undergone but very little change since he was 'a herd on Yarrow.' His face and hands are still as brown as if he lived entirely *sub dio*. His very hair has a coarse stringiness about it, which proves beyond dispute its utter ignorance of all the arts of the friseur; and hangs in playful whips and cords about his ears, in a style of the most perfect innocence imaginable. His mouth, which, when he smiles, nearly cuts the totality of his face in twain, is an object that would make the Chevalier Ruspini die with indignation; for his teeth have been allowed to grow where they listed, and as they listed, presenting more resemblance, in arrangement, (and colour too,) to a body of crouching sharp-shooters, than to any more regular species of array . . . .

As for the Burns's dinner, I really cannot in honesty pretend to give you any very exact history of the latter part of its occurrences. As the night kept advancing, the company kept diminishing, till about one o'clock in the morning, when we found ourselves reduced to a small staunch party of some five-and-twenty, men not to be shaken from their allegiance to King Bacchus, by any changes in his administration — in other words, men who by no means considered it as necessary to leave the room, because one, or even because two presidents had set them such an example. The last of these presidents, Mr Patrick Robertson, a young counsellor of very rising reputation and most pleasant manners, made his approach to the chair amidst such a thunder of acclamation as seems to be issuing from the cheeks of the Bacchantes, when Silenus gets astride on his ass, in the famous picture of Rubens. Once in the chair, there was no fear of his quitting it while any remained to pay homage due to his authority. He made speeches, one chief merit of which consisted (unlike Epic poems) in their having neither beginning, middle, nor end. He sung songs in which music was not. He proposed toasts in which meaning was not — But over everything that he said there was flung such a radiance of sheer mother-wit, that there was no difficulty in seeing the want of *meaning* was no involuntary want. By the perpetual dazzle of his wit, by the cordial flow of his good humour, but above all, by the cheering influence of his broad happy face, seen through its halo of punch-steam (for even the chair had by this time got enough of the juice of the grape,) he contrived to diffuse over us all, for a long time, one genial atmosphere of unmingled mirth. How we got out of that atmosphere, I cannot say I remember.

Peter's Letters to his Kinsfolk

James Boswell

Very Grave though Much Intoxicated

This extract from Boswell's journals for the years immediately following his famous tour of the Hebrides with Dr Johnson gives a further airing to one of his constant preoccupations — drinking. Clearly, in his mid-thirties, his capacity was still prodigious. This volume was edited by Charles Ryscamp and F.J. Pottle.

THURSDAY 3 NOVEMBER [1774]. After breakfast Lord Alva, Mr Barclay Maitland, and the rest of the freeholders for Captain Erskine came, and we went to Clackmannan in goodly form with I forget how many carriages. I was introduced to Colonel Masterton, whom I had never seen before. General Scott was made praeses, and appeared as a sensible, respectable man of good family and great property. But it was an odd reflection that his great distinction was owing to his having been a professed gamester. We returned to Alloa and had a grand dinner. Fortune's cook and Steele the confectioner and his man were brought from Edinburgh. The family of Mar, though by accident defeated in the county (supposing a petition to the House of Commons not to succeed), appeared with becoming magnificence. So many of us drank from dinner till ten at night, when we were told supper was on the table. We had no ladies with us today. I was in high spirits, supped voraciously, drank more after it, but had reason enough to go to bed while I could walk.

FRIDAY 4 NOVEMBER. Colonel Campbell and I set out in his chaise about eight. I was not much indisposed. We breakfasted at the North Ferry, stopped at Queensferry, and drank a glass at Bailie Buncle's; drove to town, and came out of our chaise at the Exchange, that all who were at the Cross might see us after our victory. I went home and saw my wife and Veronica, then dined with the Colonel at his lodgings, and, as he was to be busy, just drank half a bottle of port; then sallied forth between four and five with an avidity for drinking from the habit of some days before. I went to Fortune's; found nobody in the house but Captain James Gordon of Ellon. He and I drank five bottles of claret and were most profound politicians. He pressed me to take another; but my stomach was against it. I walked off very gravely though much intoxicated. Ranged through the streets till, having run hard down the Advocates' Close, which is very steep, I found myself on a sudden bouncing down an almost perpendicular stone stair. I could not stop, but when I came to the bottom of it, fell with a good deal of violence, which sobered me much. It was amazing that I was not killed or very much hurt; I only bruised my right heel severely. I supped at Sir George's. My wife was there, and George Webster.

The Ominous Years, 1774−76

Ian McGinness

In the Public Bar

This is Glasgow in the 1980s. The sketches of Glasgow life which make up the book from which this extract is taken are done with disillusioned clarity. The city is explored through the eyes of three disaffected characters: a disgruntled teacher, a drunken car worker and an office worker leading a double life. In his introduction to the novel, published in 1987, McGinness says that this is 'a book about looking into the eyes of a dead dog and seeing the world reflected in watery glass.'

Gerry popped from the car and the three experienced hands burst into the maelstrom of the public bar. Feverish customers stood three-deep at the counter, raising fists which clenched five pound and single notes, hoarsely imploring the harassed bar staff for service as the minutes of their lunch break ticked away. Many were from the plant; others wore the muddied boots and wellingtons of building site workers. Standing quietly around the edge, nursing warm dregs, were the pinched faces of the bar flies, vainly hoping to cadge drinks from old or new acquaintances.

Suddenly, Gerry leapt into the air like Denis Law in full flight, seeming to hover in the air as his head snap-panned left to right to determine who was serving behind the bar. Landing back on his feet, he nudged Pat with his elbow: 'Watch this,' he advised. A second salmon leap took him into unobstructed space, and at the highest point of the jump he shouted over the heads of the wriggling, elbowing crowd: 'Three pints of lager, Rita!'

A few heads at the back of the mob turned round and several muffled curses were heard, but time was too short to grudge other people their influence. Gerry held out his hands to the grumblers in mock supplication: 'Can I help it if the girl finds me sexually attractive, boys? Now can I?'

'Has she still got a fancy for you?' asked Danny in amazement. 'After you giving her a dizzy last week?'

Gerry shrugged his shoulders: 'It's just animal magnetism, boys, that's all. Anyway, they like being mistreated a wee bit. It gets them drooling.'

'Is that why you fuck the wife about then?' asked Pat. Danny nudged his arm and looked away.

'Pat, Pat,' said Gerry calmly, with a hint of menace glistening beneath the surface like a shard of steel reflecting sunlight. 'That's uncalled for. Don't you think so, Dan?'

'Come on now, boys,' said Danny soothingly, his podgy hands smoothing the air. 'Don't let's start all this again. We're here for a wee drink.' At this point, a beringed female hand appeared above the heads in the crowd and an index finger pointed towards the right-hand side of the pub. 'Helloooh!' announced Danny triumphantly, 'we're off!'

The three men fought their way through the throng to an oasis of calm beside the food counter where there was no bar staff and no beer pumps. There, Rita was waiting with three pints of lager. Gerry flashed a grin on his dark, still youthful face, showing white teeth which enhanced his slyly attractive features. He stroked his moustache like someone he had once seen on television:

'Rita, my wee beauty,' he said throatily, extending his right hand to clasp hers.

'Don't you come near me, Gerry Mulhearn,' snapped Rita, slapping his hand aside. 'What happened to you last week? I waited over an hour for you and you never showed.'

'Come here, pet,' said Gerry, gesturing her towards him.

'No, I'm not coming near you. That's it as far as I'm concerned.'

'Come here,' Gerry coaxed, now leaning on the bar towards her. 'I just want to have a wee word in your ear.'

Rita feigned a look of displeasure then tilted her blonde head in his direction: 'All right, then. But I don't know why I'm listening.'

Gerry bent towards her ear and his tongue darted out, briefly licking the lobe, eliciting a muffled giggle from Rita. He whispered a few words and at the same time his right hand crept over the bar in a wide outflanking movement, slowly moving closer to Rita's ample backside, coated in a second skin of lime green satin. Suddenly his hand darted forwards, goosing Rita, who leapt into the air roaring with laughter. She slapped his wrist for the second time and moved off towards the other customers, darting a knowing look in his direction as she went: 'I'll believe you,' she said as her parting shot, 'thousands wouldn't.'

'Rita!' shouted Gerry at her retreating back. 'Three half pints this time; and three halfs!' By this time both Pat and Danny were fingering glasses which had barely a trace of lager at the bottom, so Gerry placed his pint to his lips and drained three quarters of the contents: 'See that?' he asked, gesturing with his thumb over his shoulder. 'It's the old magic touch. Don't you wish you were in the super stud bracket, Pat?'

'She's a hell of a brainy lassie, isn't she?' mused Danny, scratching his ear.

'Fantastic, Danny,' replied Pat. 'There's miles of unexplored territory inside her head, just waiting to be discovered.'

'Who's bothering about the grey matter?' asked Gerry incredulously.

'Look at the body it's got on it. She's some fucking ride, I'll tell you that for nothing.'

'Is that right?' asked Pat innocently. 'I noticed you didn't bother to pay for the pints. Is that you starting to rent your prick out now?'

Gerry's dark features whitened slightly as he drained the rest of his lager: 'We've just got a wee arrangement, that's all,' he said softly. 'You've been known to borrow money before, haven't you, Pat?'

'Not from women, Gerry.'

'Oh, sorry, I thought you did. I must have been getting it mixed up with your kids' Christmas present money.'

Pat slammed the empty glass on the bar.

'Boys, boys,' pleaded Danny. 'I thought this was all finished between you two! For Christ's sake, I'm down here for a quiet drink, and if you're going to ruin it for me I'm going to fuck off and the both of you can hike it back to the plant. Look,' he said, gesturing towards the counter, 'there's Rita with the bevvy.' Rita set down a tray on the bar and placed six glasses before them. Three were half pint mugs containing lager, three tot glasses containing whisky.

'You're a wee darling, Rita,' said Gerry. Rita flashed a brief smile:

'That'll be two pounds, ten pence.'

'I'll get it,' said Pat, fumbling in his pocket.

'No, hold on,' argued Danny.

'Here, I'll get it,' insisted Pat, handing over three pounds. 'Get one yourself, Rita.'

'Thanks, pet.'

'Get us three halfs when you're ready, darling, will you?' asked Danny.

'OK.'

All three men drained their whisky glass and poured the dregs into the lager.

'Where the fuck's that brother of mine?' demanded Gerry.

'The boy's just as well not coming in here in his first week anyway,' counselled Danny.

'But he's supposed to be coming out for a drink with me. I told him I'd show him about. Daft wee cunt. He's off his fucking head, anyway. He's been going with the same lemon since he was fourteen: the wee prick. He's going to get married and he's only shagged one woman. Sometimes I think he hasn't even screwed the one he's going with.'

'He's just a young boy,' interposed Pat.

'Oh yes, a lot you know about it, Casanova. I've heard all about you.'

'Leave off, Gerry, will you?' pleaded Danny. 'Here's the drinks, anyway. Cheers. What's the damage?'

'One thirty-five.'

'There you are.'

'That's it exact. Thank you.'

'Don't mention it.'

'Another three halfs, Rita, eh?' asked Gerry.

'I don't think we've got time,' said Danny doubtfully. 'What do you think, Pat?'

'Oh, fuck it. Let him get them.'

All three men drained their whisky glass and poured the dregs into the lager.

Gerry stretched and belched loudly over the heads of his two companions. He rocked off the bar: 'I'm away for a slash,' he explained. 'Don't worry, Pat,' he continued as he brushed past on his way to the toilet. 'I won't ask you to pay for it: it's on me.'

'Great, Gerry. That's a big relief. I'm not used to being out with such monied company.' Then, as Gerry disappeared into the toilet, releasing a draught of stale urine: 'Fucking prick!'

'Take it easy, Pat,' warned Danny, placing a soothing hand on his elbow.

'He just gets on my tits, Danny, that's all. What the fuck do you bring him along for, anyway? We used to have good wee bevvies along here: me and George and you, before George got pumped. I know he's your wife's brother, but enough's enough. And now I see we've got two of them.'

'Come on, now. Wee Liam's OK.'

'Maybe so, but I suppose Gerry was like that once too. Where's the wee cunt got to anyway?'

Danny looked furtively over his shoulder: 'I told him not to come into the pub.'

'What? Jesus, if Gerry knew that ... What the fuck did you do that for?'

'You know what can happen, Pat. The boy's only just starting. Let him find his feet first, then he can decide which side of the fence he's on for himself.'

'Do you know, Danny, you're a big soft bastard at heart, aren't you? Always keeping the peace. What would we do without you, eh?'

'Laugh if you want, Pat, but I'll tell you one thing: sometimes I can go home at night and know I've done something good. You know, something really good, not just putting some fucking bolt in the right place.'

'Take it easy, big man; I know, I know.'

'Do you fuck, Pat. I'll tell you something: all you know is what you find at the bottom of these glasses, and it's showing.'

'Come on now, Danny, cool it down.'

'And I'll tell you another thing,' continued Danny, laying a finger on Pat's chest as he again glanced behind him at the creaking toilet door. 'Lay off the snide with Gerry. You know he can be an evil bastard. You've talked to Margaret.'

'And I've seen her too,' interjected Pat. 'I've seen her on Sunday mornings with the dark glasses on to hide the black eyes.'

'Well, just leave it out. I want none of it today.'

Pat shrugged his shoulders and tilted the lager glass to his mouth, gulping the contents with a gasp of contentment: 'At least we know where the money comes from to let Rita buy all of those drinks.'

'What do you mean?'

Pat lifted his glass to eye level and shook the remaining inch of lager from side to side: 'I haven't got any change back from my round yet.'

Danny tilted his head back and laughed, the flesh on his throat and jowls shaking in waves: 'Poor Pat. Fuck all's working out for you these days, is it?'

The toilet door slammed and Danny furtively snapped a look over his shoulder: 'Remember.'

'No drinks yet?' shouted Gerry questioningly, slapping Danny solidly on his upholstered back: 'Rita!'

'Coming!'

Rita wobbled up to the bar carrying three whiskies. Gerry blew her a kiss as he searched for his glass: 'You're a marvel, girl, a fucking marvel. Did anyone ever tell you?'

'Yes.'

All three men drained their whisky glass and poured the dregs into the lager. With an automaton movement, Danny threw the beer down his throat:

'Come on, let's make a move. We've about thirty seconds to make it back to the chain gang.'

Outside the pub they found Liam leaning against the car, systematically destroying a packet of salt 'n' vinegar crisps.

'Where the fuck have you been?' demanded Gerry, staring into his brother's eyes before he thrust him aside and pulled open the car door.

'Looking after Danny's car.'

'What?' asked Gerry incredulously, staring at him again as he paused before he climbed into the back seat.

'Looking after Danny's car,' repeated Liam. 'He didn't lock it.'

'Jesus Christ!' exclaimed Gerry as he threw himself in. He gestured with an index finger: 'Get in, cunt face. Come on and throw these fucking things out!' As he screamed his last instruction, he grabbed Liam's crisp bag and threw it on to the pavement as the boy squirmed in beside him. 'I can't stand the smell of those things.'

Liam settled in beside his brother, his legs cramped submissively in response to Gerry's assertive, splaying knees. He stared silently through the side window as his bony hands again found their way into blue-white gloves.

Halfway to the factory Gerry began to hum a tune, and after a few seconds he was accompanied by Liam who drummed his fingers clumsily on the back of the seat, glancing apprehensively towards his brother. In the front of the car Pat hummed half of a bar then broke into song:

'Her eyes, they shone like diamonds,
They called her the queen of the land,
And her hair hung over her shoulders,
Tied up with a black velvet band.'

Danny joined in the next verse, gently harmonising, and the song continued until the car pulled in through the factory gates. No one spoke as the car doors were slammed. Each individual hurriedly made for his own particular entrance into the complex, each swallowed up, vanishing like a pebble on the beach. It was Monday afternoon: only eight shopping days until Christmas.

Inner City

George Outram

The Banks o' the Dee

I met wi' a man on the banks o the Dee,
And a merrier body I never did see;
Though Time had bedrizzled his haffits wi' snaw,
An' Fortune had stown his luckpenny awa',
Yet never a mortal mair happy could be
Than the man that I met on the banks o the Dee.

When young, he had plenty o owsen an' kye,
A wide wavin' mailin, an' siller forbye;
But cauld was his hearth ere his youdith was o'er,
An' he delved on the lands he had lairdit before;
Yet though beggared his ha' an' deserted his lea,
Contented he roamed on the banks o the Dee.

'Twas heartsome to see the auld body sae gay,
As he toddled adoun by the gowany brae,
Sae canty, sae crouse, an' sae proof against care;
Yet it wasna through riches, it wasna through lear;
But I fand out the cause ere I left the sweet Dee —
The man was as drunk as a mortal could be!

Clifford Hanley

More Precious than Gold

Clifford Hanley's book, *Dancing in the Streets*, from which this
extract comes, was first published in 1958. It is a classic account of
a Glasgow childhood in the 1920s and 1930s.

For a real Glasgow drunk, if he doesn't want a fight, wants to give his
money away. That's why they love Glaswegians in Blackpool and the Isle
of Man. The English industrialist may tip sixpence and the American
millionaire may put a comptometer on the bill to check mistakes in addition, but the Glaswegian on a spree wants rid of the filthy stuff. When
the genuine Glasgow keelie steps off the train or the boat in Glasgow
after his holidays, he thinks he has cheated somebody if he has enough
in his pocket to pay his tram fare home.

And the drunks *did* give pennies away. They swayed on the corners
and dug into their pockets for more pennies. Jimmie said that their wives
needed those pennies to buy food for their children, and I didn't want to
have their children starved, but I did feel that if the pennies were being
handed out and the kids would starve anyway, I might as well have a
penny as anybody else. That was before I discovered where Jimmie had
picked up all this inside stuff about liquor. The Band of Hope, of course.

You can't have Glasgow without that because it illustrates one of the
truths about the Glaswegian: he takes a mad breenge at everything he
goes for. Glasgow drinking is savage and Glasgow temperance is prac-
tically lethal and it's hard to say which one is the cause of the other.

Jackie and Jimmie took me to the Band of Hope, in the Wesleyan hall
in Wesleyan Street, and I got my first year's membership card and my
first stamp on it. Without the membership card and a good show of attendance stamps you were kept out of the annual dumpling night at
Christmas. Well do I remember the stunned, incredibly innocent faces
of the rejected on dumpling night — most of them gatecrashers from
other branches or the Chapel or England, even.

We sat at the back and joined in the hymn, an old Band of Hope
favourite — 'Dare to Be a Daniel, Dare to stand alone', and a very useful
watchword for five-year-olds in Glasgow. It meant that no matter how

much your school pals joshed you, you had to look noble and skip your turn at the whisky and soda.

> 'Dare to have a purple film
> And dare to make it known',

Jimmie sang.

'What's a purple film?' I asked him, fascinated.

'It's in the hymn. I'll show you it next week.'

Next week I caught on. They had a magic lantern and a dim purple light shone out at the back of it all the time it was performing. But I still couldn't see what Daniel wanted a purple film for.

After the hymns and prayers the Band of Hope put on the main event. Many of these star turns stick out in my recollection, because even after we moved away from Gallowgate Jimmie and I kept going to another thing called the Guild of Honour, which was exactly the same as the Band of Hope except that it sounded higher-class and less proley.

The routine entertainment was a visiting speaker with a cute kind of title for his lecture, like 'More Precious than Gold' (water) or 'The Secret Enemy' (alcohol). Some brought anatomical charts to unroll and pictures of human tripes and cirrhosed liver sections, and so on, the kind of thing that interests toddlers to under-tens. Some of them didn't altogether grip their audiences, and the Band of Hope was a noisy kind of evening, but not so noisy as when the arrangements broke down and a speaker didn't appear. We had all the peevish impatience of a Roman arena crowd when the Christians have been withheld. All the same, I took everything in with passionate fixity. They didn't have to work hard on me — I was their boy from the first hand-coloured liver section I met. The first rumblings of disaffection didn't stir in my mind until the man with the water speech, which was years after my initiation.

He was a good enough performer, a bit on the thin nasal side vocally but fast and slick and well able to shut hecklers up without any help from the chairman's gong. But he was just obsessed with water. He wasn't satisfied to take the traditional swipe at alcohol — *any* liquid except pure water was a fraud according to this fish. Tea was an insidious drug; coffee a rampant poison; cocoa an innocent enough thing in itself but dangerous and futile because, in making cocoa, you actually *boiled the purity out of the water*. You could see that given half a chance he would turn against water itself and leave us nothing to drink except saliva. I got so fed up with water that I finished up de-converted.

Dancing in the Streets

John Galt

Good for the Cholera

John Galt (1779–1839) may have been better known for his novels, or 'theoretical histories' as he preferred them to be known (see the extract from one of his finest, *The Provost*, page 000), but his acute observations of small-town society and politics are no less enjoyable in his shorter pieces. This passage is taken from 'Our Borough', included in the selection edited by Ian A. Gordon, his biographer.

Having been thus disappointed in the ploy of a deputation to London, by the manoeuvre described, which was no doubt a machination, there was not a member of the corporation that did not feel himself, all the rest of the day, in a state of uncertainty and tribulation. Those of the enemy's camp not expecting such a result, were afraid, not knowing what to make of it, that some hidden danger was in their triumph; and for our side, we saw that the whole affair was just a' nonsense, and would not be productive of any good, there being neither common sagacity nor a right understanding among those who made themselves cock-sure of the jaunt. But towards the afternoon we grew more composed, for the Provost, a regardful man, sent round one of the town-officers to tell us that we would be glad to hear it was not the Cholera which made him so danger-. ous. 'In short,' said Sunday, as the town-officer was called by the weans, in sport, 'he has just had a touch of the molly-grubs, which the leddy has pacified with rhubarb and brandy, and he'll be weel enough at night.'

Those that had discernment among us, were at no loss how to construe this message; and I accordingly went by myself, about eight o'clock, to his house, for I was very much consoled to hear the Provost had but suffered from a false alarm, and would, in the end, be the better of his dose of physic.

Going at eight o'clock, I found Past-Bailie Drivel there before me, who, though an old man and sorely failed, was not without a name for corporation business. He had heard who had been named for the deputation, and in what manner, and was, like every body of common sense, demented that it should have been so.

'But thanks be and praise,' said he, 'when we spoke anent it, the sederunt has been no sederunt at all — no minutes have been written out — the Provost's calamity put a stop to the business, and he has only

to plead — which he can well do — that he was not in a capacity to preside, and therefore the meeting must stand a *dies non*, as it is called in the Latin language, in which these words signify no meeting at all.'

'Really, Bailie,' said the Provost himself, as he sat in his easy-chair with his wife's shawl over his shoulders, a cod behind his back, and on his head a clean white cotton nightcap, 'Really, Bailie, ye have thought my very thought — for, as sure as death, I was in no condition to argol bargol with any body, and ought — so great was my all-overishness — to have dismissed the Council before we came to the vote, and now that I think on't, the whole affair passed as a matter of course, without coming to a vote at all — It was just a kind of a hear and say.'

'Na,' said Mr Drivel, 'if that's the case we're all safe yet. Ye must just insist on making a *dies non* — and if I were you, and you had my experience, I would have no meeting at all — but say that it was an unregularity altogether.'

'But if we make a new 'lection for the deputation, the Reformers may again come on our blind side, and play another souple trick.'

Ah, Provost, ye must not let them — just there where ye sit, in all the parapharnauly of a patient at death's door — send word to the Town Treasurer, that although Providence has been pleased to take you from your duty at this time, yet it has left you your head, and therefore as the business to London cannot wait, ye will dispatch the Dean of Guild forthwith on your own responsibility — ordering him to be supplied with money. And what's to hinder you, Mr Dean of Guild,' said he, turning to me, 'when ye're in London, to write down to us that ye cannot do without help, and then we'll send up to you those we know will be agreeable? Odd's sake, Provost, it was a very convenient stroke of policy to fall sick of such an outstrapolous malady as the cholera, so nicely in the nick of time.' — And Bailie Drivel rubbed his hands with fainness.

Just as we were thus soberly discoursing, another of the Council came in. He was one that we were not quite sure of, for on more than one occasion we had seen in him a leaning to the Radical side — and we could not divine what had brought him, for the Provost, as he afterwards told me himself, had most particularly directed Sunday to call only on our own friends. But it turned out that Mrs Canny, the councillor's wife, being vogie that her gudeman was in the way to be a bailie, always gave Sunday a dram when he came with a message on town business, and the pawkie bodie none doubting his reward, thought he could not do better than take the blithe tidings of the Provost's recovery to her door. Howsoever, the Provost fell into a low fit soon after Mr Canny came in, and as he could not carry on the discourse, particularly anent the town business, and the intruder was not on a familiarity with him, we soon got rid of that thorn in the flesh, and Past-Bailie Drivel with me, we stayed behind.

Presently the Provost brightened up, and bade us make another tumbler, and Mr Drivel, as he was brewing his, and brizzing the sugar with the mahogany bruizer, looked out over his tumbler from aneath his brows, and said to the Provost with a pyet's eyes, 'I have heard brandy commended as a medicine for the cholera.'

'So have I,' said the Provost, 'and if our friend the Dean of Guild doesna think it will do me harm, I dare say I could take a thimbleful.'

'Harm!' cried I; 'far be sic a thought from me — it's a medicine — and surely a medicine ought to do you good.'

Whereupon he drew his tumbler towards him, syne the gardivine, and made a cheerer that would have shamed to paleness the water of a tanhole.

'Eh! what am I about?' said he; 'but, Bailie, ye say that brandy's good for the cholera?'

'If ye hae't,' quoth the old man, again rubbing his hands, as if the palms had been kittly, drawing his under lip shavlingly over his upper, with a keckling kind of a laugh, that was funnier to thole than an advocate's pun.

Being thus restored to our ease and composure, though we did count on some others of our party coming in, we had a solid crack anent the signs of the times, for the London paper of that evening seemed to speak very ominously; no longer giving us that heartening to stand out against the reform which behoved an organ of the Government to do.

'Aye,' said the Provost, 'that is a sign! things are come to a pretty pass now. We are really cast upon an awful time. The nation's in a boiling confusion. Scum, pease, and barley are all walloping through ither. It is full time that we were on our posts; when, Dean of Guild, will ye be in a condition to go? Our hearths and altars are at stake.'

'The ashes of our ancestors,' cried Bailie Drivel.

'All that's dear to us,' said I.

'Yes,' replied the Provost, with solemnity, 'all is at stake, and the man who will not make a stand in this monstrous crisis, is a very worthless person.'

'But in what way,' cried I, 'is the stand to be made? I am ready.'

'So am I,' said the Bailie.

'The Radicals are up! the Whigs are up! and the Tories are crying for the mountains to fall on them,' said the Provost.

In short, we all worked ourselves into a consternation, in so much, that before old Bailie Drivel was half done with his toddy, his heart filled full, and the tear rushed into his eye in a very pitiful manner. But still we had between hands some sober conversation, and agreed among ourselves, that before manifesting at that time any change, or shadow of change, in our councils, it behoved me to set off for London, and write the Provost what was the signs and aspects of the times in London. And, accordingly, after a very serious sederunt, we parted for the night, and I went home to my own house.

'Our Borough', in *Selected Short Stories*

Peter Mackenzie

The Dram-Drinking Case

The pursuer in this other notable case, set forth in his summons of damages (either prepared by A.M. or H.B.), that having quietly gone into a dram-shop in Nile Lane on a Saturday in September, 1822, 'he was soon afterwards followed or joined by the defender, who forthwith proceeded without any just cause or provocation whatsoever, (*sic orig.*) to throw the whole contents of a glass of whisky in his, the pursuer's face, which having touched his right eye, it produced a violent inflammation, *and the pursuer was thereby deprived of his vision in the said eye.*' He therefore sought £100 of damages from the defender, besides the expenses of process, etc.

In his defence (prepared by P.A. or J.W.), it was stated and explained that the defender was *a very young man*, (*sic orig.*), and had *lately* got himself married, and that it was not true that he had followed the pursuer into the house in question; but on the contrary that the pursuer followed him and some of his wedding friends or companions; that he was not long seated when the pursuer placed a glass of whisky before the defender, which he insisted should be swigged off at once; that the defender might willingly have done so, but he perceived that there was a *mawk* or maggot at the bottom of the said glass, and not having any particular relish for mawks or maggots (*sic orig.*), he refused to drink the whole of the contents of the said glass of whisky, whereupon the pursuer not only *damned* him as a surly person, but uttered many unwarrantable insinuations and expressions such as, that he had kissed the defender's newly-made wife at a recent ball in the Waterloo Tavern, and that she had dropped her handkerchief to him at a reel of '*Babbity bowster*' in Fraser's well-known assembly rooms in King Street; which unfounded allegations or insinuations so provoked the defender in his newly-married condition that he threw a little of the whisky 'into the pursuer's foresaid eye.' The defender, however, averred that no such small quantity of spirits could produce anything like inflammation as alleged in the summons, but that a small quantity of *snuff* besides, was thrown '*into the eye in question,*' in a minute or two afterwards by some other person, for whom the defender was not answerable.

On advising the procedure, the Sheriff-Substitute ordained the pursuer to give in a condescendence of the facts he offered to prove in support of his libel, and allowed the defender to answer the same. Thereafter, a long *proof* was adduced by both parties, on advising which, his lordship disposed of this *'very important case'* (as it was called), by the following remarkable judgment, and here we also close this short chapter —

'Having advised the proof adduced by both parties, with certificate of circumduction against the pursuer, and note for the defender renouncing farther probation, holds the proof as concluded, and finds that on the occasion in question, *the parties were in good humour with one another* (*sic orig.*), until the pursuer addressed the irritating expressions mentioned in the proof as applicable to his wife, to whom the defender (*a young man*), had recently been married, in consequence of which expressions the defender, *from the impulse of the moment*, threw some whisky from a glass in the pursuer's face, part of which went into one of his eyes, and that the pursuer complained at the time that *he felt as if there was a mote in his eye:* Finds that the witness, Anthony Davidson, having been requested to assist in relieving the pursuer's eye from the mote which he thought was in it, put some *snuff* into the said eye: Finds that the pursuer was off his work for several days after the transaction, and apparently from the injury which his said eye had sustained, but whether from the whisky or the snuff or partly from both has not been proved: Finds that the pursuer has not led any proof in support of the third article of his condescendence, or that part of the fourth article which bears that he has been obliged to pay large sums to his medical attendants, or even that he took any medical advice whatever, on the subject in question: Finds that it was from the misconduct of the pursuer himself that the occurrence betwixt him and the defender originally took place, and on the whole facts and circumstances of the case assoilzies the defender from the conclusion of the action, and decerns, reserving consideration of the point of expenses.'

Reminiscences of Glasgow

Robert Burns

The Virtues of Drink

These stanzas are taken from 'The Holy Fair', one of the finest poems in the collection which brought Burns such immediate, overwhelming success on its appearance in 1786, *Poems Chiefly in the Scottish Dialect*. This poem's title refers to the great outdoor communion service where preaching, drinking and flirting went on simultaneously.

Now, butt an' ben, the Change-house fills,
  Wi' *yill-caup* Commentators:
Here's crying out for bakes an' gills,
  An' there, the pint-stowp clatters;
While thick an' thrang, an' loud an' lang,
  Wi' *Logic*, an' wi' *Scripture*,
They raise a din, that, in the end,
  Is like to breed a rupture
    O' wrath that day.

Leeze me on Drink! it gies us mair
  Than either School or Colledge:
It kindles Wit, it waukens Lear,
  It pangs us fou o' Knowledge.
Be't *whisky-gill* or *penny-wheep*,
  Or onie stronger potion,
It never fails, on drinkin deep,
  To kittle up our *notion*,
    By night or day.

The lads an' lasses, blythely bent
  To mind baith *saul* an' *body*,
Sit round the table, weel content,
  An' steer about the *Toddy*.
On this ane's dress, an' that ane's leuk,
  They're makin observations;
While some are cozie i' the neuk,
  An' forming *assignations*
    To meet some day....

How monie hearts this day converts,
    O' Sinners and o' Lasses!
Their hearts o' stane, gin night are gane
    As saft as ony flesh is.
There's some are fou o' *love divine*;
    There's some are fou o' *brandy*;
An' monie jobs that day begin,
    May end in *Houghmagandie*
        Some ither day.

'The Holy Fair,' in
Poems Chiefly in the Scottish Dialect

Glossary

Aboon above
Ackie active (?)
A gey wheen a good number
Aiblins perhaps
Ask newt
A wad in pledge

Bauld strong, healthy, bold
Bee-skep beehive
Beikit me warmed myself
Bicker drinking vessel
Blellum babbler
Bowster bolster
Bowster cup pillow cup or nightcap
Brans calf (of leg)
Bree sauce (*barley bree* = whisky or ale)
Browster brewer
Buckie obstinate person
Butt and ben in both the outer and inner room

Cairfull dyte sad composition
Camstarle quarrelsome
Cantie cheerful
Canty see *Cantie*
Capernoitie bad-tempered
Capie ale
Carline, carling woman
Cauler fresh
Ceilidh (gaelic) informal social gathering with singing and story-telling
Chapman billies merchant fellows
Close entrance to tenement
Closemouth entrance to a close (see above)
Coof fool
Cornkist storage bin for corn
Cosh fool
Counter-loupers shopmen

Coup overthrown
Coupin' upending
Cowt a rough, awkward person
Craig neck
Craize infirm
Creeshy greasy
Crippen creeping
Crouse cheerful

Died dune dead beat
Deoch-an'-doris stirrup-cup
Divor ne'er do well
Donnert stupid
Doolie dreary, dismal
Douce respectable, comfortable
Dowf sad
Dowie sad, gloomy
Draipie drop
Drappikie drop (of liquor)
Dreich dreary
Drouthy thirsty

Elbuck elbow
Elriche elf-like, fairy, strange

Fairins deserts
Fankles becomes clumsy
Fecht fight
Feck most
Fleer mock
Flesher butcher
Forbye besides
Fou drunk
Fozy ragged, frayed

Gabie mouth
Gait way
Gar make
Gear possessions
Gend simple
Gin if

Gleg quick
Gliff look at hurriedly, frighten
Gowany covered with daisies
Greit wept
Gulphs profound depths

Haffits side-locks
Hairst harvest
Hap good fortune
Harns brains
Haurl pull
Heich skeich high-spirited
Herbry lodging
Hobbleshow uproar, tumult
Hoolie moderately
Hough back of the thigh
Houghmagandie fornication

Ilk, ilka each, every
Ingle chimney, hearth

Jalouse suspect, suppose

Keek peep
Kerk care, anxiety
Kell woman's head-dress
Kimmer (cummer) gossip,
   woman friend
Kir wanton
Kittle tickle, excite
Knagie peg
Kye cows
Kyth appear

Lauching laughing
Leer learning
Leez me on I am very fond of
Leuch laughed
Libbit castrate
Limmer loose woman
Loup leap
Loupit up leapt up
Lum chimney

Mailin farm rent
Mawk maggot
Melder meal-grinding
Muckle much

Nappy ale
Neb face
Neep turnip
Neist next

Neuk corner
Niffer banter, haggle

Orra man odd-job man
Ourtane overtaken
Owsen oxen
Oxter armpit

Patie pot
Partan large crab
Peching wheezing
Pang cram, stuff
Penny-wheep small beer
Philabeg kilt
Pish piss
Pith strength-giving drink
Plooky covered with pimples
Puckie bag
Pycharis pitchers

Quorum company

Reaming swats foaming new ale
Reek smoke
Rigs raised strips of ploughed land
Rin the cutter carry out liquor from a
   public-house unobserved
Riz rose
Roset rub with rosin
Roppined roped
Rotten rat

Sair iced over-iced
Scantlins scarcely
Sark shirt, shift
Sheckle wrist
Shune shoes
Siller money
Skailing dispersing
Skellum good-for-nothing
Skite dart through air
Slap gap in a hedge
Smeddum energy, drive
Sneck latch
Sneck-trap trap that snaps shut
Souple supple
Souter cobbler
Speer ask
Speil climb
Steek close
Steir bustle
Stoor dust
Stramash commotion

193

Stuffie whisky
Syne then, since

Tapie top
Tash stain, deface
Thrang closely packed, busy
Tine lose
Threpit agreed
Thrapple throat
Tint lost
Tippeny cheap ale
Tither another
Tittit pulled

Tosh neat, smart
Tutie tippler
Twal' twelve

Usky whisky

Wamblet rolled
Wittens news, information

Yad old mare or horse
Yeid went
Yill-caup ale-cup
Youdith youth

Publishers' Acknowledgements

André Deutsch Ltd would like to thank the following publishers for their permission to reproduce extracts from the works indicated:

Scots Fisherfolk by Peter F. Anson (Saltire Society, 1950)

Dancing in the Streets by Clifford Hanley, © Clifford Hanley 1958. Acknowledgement is due to Curtis Brown Ltd on behalf of Clifford Hanley.

The Last Peacock by Alan Massie (The Bodley Head, 1980)

Old Wife in High Spirits and *A Drunk Man Looks at a Thistle* by Hugh MacDiarmid (*Complete Poems 1920–1976 Vol. II*, Martin Brian & O'Keefe Ltd, 1978). Acknowledgement is also due to the author's executor, Michael Grieve.

Inner City by Iain McGinness (Polygon Press, 1987)

The Big Man by William McIlvanney (Hodder and Stoughton, 1985)

Docherty by William McIlvanney, © William McIlvanney 1975 (Mainstream, 1983)

Brebster Ceilidh by David Morrison (*Hammer and Thistle* by Alan Bold and David Morrison, 1973)

The Steeple Bar by Sydney Goodsir Smith (*Collected Poems 1941–1975* (John Calder [Pubishers] Ltd, 1975)

195

A Wee Dram

Index of Contributors

Anson, Peter F.
Argyllshire Herald

Boswell, James
Burns, Robert
Burt, Edward

Chambers, Robert
Cockburn, Lord

Douglas, George

Fergusson, Robert
Foulis, Hugh
Fyffe, Will

Gaitens, Edward
Galt, John
Gibbon, Lewis Grassic
Graham, W.S.
Grant of Rothiemurchus, Elizabeth
Gunn, Neil M.

Hanley, Clifford
Henryson, Robert
Hogg, James

Kennaway, James

Lockhart, J.G.

MacDiarmid, Hugh
McGinness, Ian
McIlvanney, William
Mackenzie, Peter
Malloch, D. MacLeod
Martin, Martin
Massie, Allan
Moir, David MacBeth
Morrison, David

North, Christopher

Outram, George

Ramsay, Allan
Ramsay, Dean

Scott, Sir Walter
Smith, Sydney Goodsir
Statistical Account of Scotland
Stewart, Alexander
Strachan, David
Strang, John

Topham, Edward

*Weekly Magazine or Edinburgh
   Amusement, The*

Picture Acknowledgements

The publishers would like to thank the following for their permission to reproduce the illustrations indicated:

p.11 *Lime Kiln at Oa, Islay,* Photograph Allan Wright

p.17 *Secret Still,* courtesy of Chivas Bros Ltd.

p.19 *Portrait of Robert Burns* by Alexander Nasymth, Scottish National Portrait Gallery

p.21 *Portrait of George Smith,* courtesy of the Glenlivet Distillery

p.25 *Fisherfolk, Dunbar c. 1900,* Photograph A. and M. Folkarde

p.26 *Portrait of Robert Fergusson* by Alexander Runciman, Scottish National Portrait Gallery

p.34 *Two Men Drinking at a Table inside a Farmhouse* by Walter Geikie, National Gallery of Scotland

p.36 *Willie Brew'd a Peck o' Maut* from *Complete Works of Robert Burns* by Allan Cunningham

p.38 *Funeral, Colonsay, 1904,* © Peter MacAllister

p.41 *Oyster Cellar in Leith* by John Burnet, National Gallery of Scotland

p.44 *The Carter's Lunch* by James Howe, National Gallery of Scotland

p.51 *Portrait of Allan Ramsay,* Mansell Collection

p.55 *Globe Close, Dumfries* from *Complete Works of Robert Burns* by Allan Cunningham

p.57 *Dance of the Apprentices* by Harry Keir

p.71 *James Boswell* by George Willison, Scottish National Portrait Gallery

p.73 *Tam O'Shanter and Souter Johnney* by Walter Geikie, National Gallery of Scotland

p.78 *Tobermory,* courtesy George Washington Wilson Collection, Aberdeen University Library

p.84 *Warlight offloading at Laphroaig Distillery,* Laphroaig Distillery

p.94 *Ceilidh in a cottage kitchen,* Mansell Collection

p.101 *While we sit bousing ...* by Walter Geikie, National Gallery of Scotland

p.106 *Pub Scene* © Douglas Corrance

p.109 *Drawing of Hugh MacDiarmid* by David Foggie, © Scotsman Publications Ltd.

p.113 *Face of Glasgow,* © Douglas Corrance

p.118 *Ceilidh,* © Douglas Corrance

p.120 *Smugglers on beach,* Mansell Collection

p.124 *Highland Dance* by David Allan, National Gallery of Scotland

p.133 *Para Handy* by William Stewart, © Seanachaidh Publishing Ltd

p.145 *Fishing boats,* © Douglas Corrance

p.148 *Very Fou* by Walter Geikie, National Gallery of Scotland

p.150 *George IV at Holyrood,* by David Wilkie, National Gallery of Scotland

199